when your
child *has...*

Asperger's
Syndrome

✓ Get the Right Diagnosis

✓ Understand Treatment Options

✓ Help Your Child Cope

William Stillman
Series Editor: Vincent Iannelli, M.D.

▲**adams**media
Avon, Massachusetts

Published by
Adams Media, an F+W Publications Company
57 Littlefield Street, Avon, MA 02322. U.S.A.
www.adamsmedia.com

Contains materials adopted and abridged from *The Everything®
Parent's Guide to Children with Asperger's Syndrome* by William Stillman, Copyright © 2005 by F+W Publications, Inc.

ISBN-13: 978-1-59869-667-7
ISBN-10: 1-59869-667-X

Printed in Canada.

J I H G F E D C B A

Library of Congress Cataloging-in-Publication Data
is available from the publisher.

*This book is available at quantity discounts for bulk purchases.
For information, please call 1-800-289-0963.*

Contents

Introduction

A diagnosis of Asperger's Syndrome can be both refreshing and heartbreaking. Refreshing because you may finally have an answer for your child's differences from other children.

Why has your child struggled socially and doesn't ever seem to make friends? How come he doesn't seem as coordinated as other kids his own age? Why does he have such narrow interests and become so obsessed about certain things? And why is he so sensitive to lights and sounds that don't bother other people?

It may be because your child has Asperger's Syndrome — a type of autism. Although 'heartbreaking' may be too strong a word, parents do often have trouble coping with a diagnosis of Asperger's Syndrome.

Even once they accept the diagnosis, they may wonder why it took so long to get their child recognized as having Asperger's Syndrome if the diagnosis was delayed. They may also have trouble getting passed the fact that Asperger's is a type of autism and may be confused about possible treatments and their child's future.

When Your Child Has . . . Asperger's Syndrome is a great resource for parents who are concerned that their child might have Asperger's Syndrome and for those who have already received a diagnosis. In addition to signs and symptoms of Asperger's Syndrome, this book will give you the information you need to get your child evaluated and properly diagnosed as early as possible.

Why is there a delay in diagnosis when kids have Asperger's Syndrome? Unlike other developmental disorders, children with Asperger's don't have any language delays and usually have normal intelligence. So they may not be diagnosed until their social issues become a problem.

Children with Asperger's Syndrome may also have a delay in their diagnosis because they are first diagnosed with something else. Their narrow interests often make them seem like they have a short attention span and emotional outbursts can make them seem impulsive and hyperactive, often leading to an inappropriate diagnosis of ADHD. Hopefully, new guidelines from the American Academy of Pediatrics on the "Identification and Evaluation of Children With Autism Spectrum Disorders," will help get children with Asperger's Syndrome diagnosed at an early age. Then parents like you can learn about available treatments, discipline, getting ready for school, and what the future has in store for your child with Asperger's Syndrome, with a book like *When Your Child Has . . . Asperger's Syndrome.*

Chapter 1

Understanding the Basics

10 Things You Will Learn in this Chapter

- About Hans Asperger—the Austrian pediatrician who formally defined the syndrome.
- What the "Refrigerator Mother Theory" is.
- How genetics might play a role in Asperger's.
- What the current definition is.
- How the diagnosis has changed in the past years.
- Why there is a skyrocketing increase in the number of children identified with autism and Asperger's Syndrome.
- How to recognize a missed diagnosis.
- Recent statistics about the prevalence of the syndrome.
- How Asperger's can be misdiagnosed as another mental health experience.
- How you or your child's other parent may have Asperger's too.

A Bit of History

Asperger's Syndrome was first formally defined in 1944 by Hans Asperger, an Austrian pediatrician. Asperger studied social interactions, communication, and behavior in children with different ways of being. In 1943, he studied a group of children, mostly boys, who had difficulty interacting in socially acceptable ways. The children appeared intrinsic or self-centered—not necessarily selfish, but rather, they preferred to keep to themselves. Another common characteristic was that they were not physically adept, and were rather uncoordinated. Most experienced no cognitive delays and were, in fact, quite articulate, with a strong command of vocabulary. The children engaged in repetitive physical actions, or were fascinated with nuances of timetables or the mechanics of certain objects such as clocks.

Asperger's in the Past

Asperger published his findings in a paper titled "Autistic Psychopathy." By today's standards, the title is alarming and disrespectful but, in using the word "psychopathy," Asperger did not intend to describe mentally ill, violent behavior; he was using the clinically acceptable jargon of the day. Asperger's findings were the first documented collection of traits now used to diagnose Asperger's Syndrome.

Unknown to Asperger, a psychiatrist named Leo Kanner was conducting similar research at Johns Hopkins University at about the same time. In 1943, Kanner chose the word "autism" (from the Greek word *autos,* or "self") to describe a group of children who shared like, but stereotyped, personality traits, engaged in solitary actions, and who struggled with expressing communication that was effective, reliable, and understandable. In postwar Austria, Asperger's paper languished while Kanner's research received recognition.

DID YOU KNOW?

Hans Asperger's findings were published nearly simultaneously with the research of Leo Kanner, another doctor who, in 1944, first distinguished the traits of autism. The two physicians were unknown to one another. Because Asperger's paper was published in German, and Kanner's in English, Kanner's research received broader distribution and was subsequently popularized. Hans Asperger passed away in 1980 before his research was universally applied.

Autism Spectrum Explained

Despite the growing recognition of autism as an acceptable diagnosis during the 1950s and 1960s, Hans Asperger's research went largely unnoticed. Still, there were individuals who experienced autistic-like symptoms but did not have the cognitive differences usually found in those with autism. At the time, such individuals were diagnosed with mental illness or nervous anxiety. Some were institutionalized or imprisoned because of their odd behavior or because they were gullible and easily manipulated into making poor or dangerous choices.

The "Refrigerator Mother Theory"

A popular theory to explain the alleged distance felt between parents, mothers in particular, and their children with autism was similarly applied to those with autistic-like symptoms. It was called "Refrigerator Mother Theory," which referred to the supposed aloofness or indifference shown by mothers unable to connect with their children. This theory reinforced the notion that mothers deliberately induced Asperger's in their children—when in fact, Asperger's Syndrome is no one's fault.

How Do Genetics Play a Role?

Some recent theories being researched to explain the prevalence of autism and Asperger's Syndrome include genetics, environmental factors (pregnant mothers' exposure to or ingestion of chemical elements), or children's reactions to the mercury preservative in certain childhood vaccinations. There is currently no prenatal or other biological exam to test for Asperger's Syndrome.

It wasn't until 1981 that British psychiatrist Lorna Wing revived Hans Asperger's findings in a research paper of her own. This eventually led to the reclassification of autistic experiences in the clinical document titled *Diagnostic and Statistical Manual of Mental Disorders* (or, as it is more commonly referred to, *DSM*).

Current Definition

The *DSM* is published in the United States by the American Psychiatric Association. As of this writing, its fourth edition, published in 1994, is still in effect. This was the first edition of the *DSM* to formally recognize Asperger's Syndrome, which was categorized under the general heading Pervasive Developmental Disorders (PDD). In addition to Asperger's, there are several other diagnoses that fall under the PDD heading. These include:

- Autistic disorder (known as autism)
- Rett disorder (or Rett Syndrome)
- Childhood disintegrative disorder
- Asperger's disorder (known as Asperger's Syndrome)
- Pervasive developmental disorder not otherwise specified (or PDD-NOS)

These are all subcategories of the PDD diagnosis. At present, these experiences are collectively grouped under the PDD heading because of the similarities of symptoms related to challenges in communication, social interaction, and so-called stereotyped behaviors, interests, and activities. Autism is the most prevalent of these experiences, more common than Down Syndrome or childhood cancer. Rett disorder is usually found in little girls before the age of four. Childhood disintegrative disorder impacts children before the age of ten. In both circumstances, and for unknown reasons, children experience a loss of previously acquired social skills, language, motor skills, play, and self-care. The category pervasive developmental disorder not otherwise specified (PDD-NOS) is used when a child demonstrates autistic-like symptoms but misses meeting the criteria for the other diagnoses.

Have You Heard the Term Highly Functional?

Some clinicians consider the terms *high-functioning autism* or *mild autism* synonymous with Asperger's Syndrome. The *DSM* does not presently define this term, so it may or may not apply to a child with Asperger's. It may also be used to describe the child who demonstrates many skills yet still falls within the PDD-NOS range of diagnosis.

PDD-NOS may be used by a physician unaccustomed to diagnosing Asperger's, or it may be used if a doctor wishes to be cautious, to "wait and see" as a child grows and develops. Sometimes, when the PDD-NOS diagnosis is revisited, a child has matured into an official Asperger's diagnosis. However, the *DSM* is a dynamic document, and as the psychiatric field grows and becomes more knowledgeable, reorganization of Asperger's and autistic experiences is inevitable in future, revised editions.

DID YOU KNOW?

Asperger's Syndrome is a neurological condition that primarily creates challenges in understanding social interactions. Asperger's is not a disease or chronic mental illness. It is a natural, lifelong experience.

Clinical Criteria

As we've learned, Asperger's Syndrome is presently grouped under the diagnostic "umbrella" heading pervasive developmental disorders, along with other disorders with similar symptoms. As currently defined by the *DSM*, a child with Asperger's differs from the child with autism because of the following traits:

- No clinically significant delays in language
- No clinically significant delays in cognitive development
- No clinically significant delays in development of age-appropriate self-help skills
- No clinically significant delays in adaptive behavior (other than social interaction)
- No clinically significant delays in curiosity about the environment in childhood

Does Your Child Qualify?

To qualify for an Asperger's Syndrome diagnosis, a child must demonstrate impairment in social interaction, shown by at least two of the following:

- Impairment in the use of nonverbal behaviors (such as eye contact, facial expressions, and gestures) during social interaction
- Lack of development of relationships with peers
- Failure to seek to share enjoyment, interests, or achievements with other people (for instance, by not showing objects of interest to others)
- Failure to reciprocate emotions or social gestures

The child should also demonstrate "restrictive repetitive and stereotyped patterns of behaviors, interests, and activities," shown by at least one of the following:

- Unusually intense preoccupation with one or
  more stereotyped interests
- Obsessively following specific, nonfunctional
  routines or rituals
- Repeated motions, such as hand or finger flapping or twisting
- Unusual preoccupation with parts of objects

To qualify as characteristics of Asperger's, these traits
must be significant enough to cause great challenges for
the child in social, occupational, and other important
areas of daily living. Although, increasingly, some children with Asperger's have been diagnosed as young as
three, the diagnosis is most often made from age six
and up.

It's Your Personal Experience

The word "disorder" may not seem like a family
friendly way to describe your child's personal Asperger's Syndrome experience, but it is currently clinical
"shorthand" to summarize it. Please do not be hurt,
confused, or upset by this technical jargon. Outside of
a doctor's office, you may wish to use the word "difference" or the phrase "different way of being" when
you feel the need to describe your child's experience,
if at all. Your child's physician, educators, or school
psychologist may be able to recommend literature in
addition to the *DSM*.

DID YOU KNOW?

The *Diagnostic and Statistical Manual* catalogs a wide range of mental health and related experiences. It is the foremost reference guide used by psychiatrists, psychologists, social workers, mental health professionals, therapists, counselors, and nurses, to name a few. It provides a framework to diagnose someone's experience according to symptoms. The first edition was originally published in 1952.

Sensory Sensitivity: Asperger's and Autism

Having just reviewed the clinical criteria for the diagnosis of Asperger's Syndrome, you may be filled with many questions and concerns. Some of what was described may match what you know to be true of your child. But you might be surprised to see that other areas weren't included. What about the child who screams and covers his ears when an ambulance goes by, blaring its siren? Or the child who cannot tolerate the taste of Jell-O or pudding in her mouth? These are called sensory sensitivities, a commonality shared with persons with autism but not defined by the DSM as clinical criteria. It is important to note that some children without Asperger's Syndrome or any medical problems at all can have some of these sensitivities too though.

Frequency of Symptoms

Your child may vibrate at a different "frequency" than most others. That is, he may be described as "exquisitely sensitive." Because of this, his entire nervous system—

his senses and emotions—may be routinely impacted by stimulation others filter out naturally.

Many children with Asperger's share some common sensitivities with people with autism. The most common sensory sensitivities are:

- Auditory (including intolerable noise or frequency levels)
- Smell and taste
- Visual
- Touch

Auditory Sensitivity

The child with exquisitely sensitive hearing may cry and recoil from a variety of sounds. She reacts in this way because in a very real sense, she is physically hurting from the intensity of the noise. The most offensive sounds are those that are not only very loud and startling but also *unpredictable*, meaning there's no telling when or where they will occur with any certainty. The most commonly hurtful, unpredictable sounds for someone with especially sensitive hearing include (in no particular order): dogs barking; babies crying; crowd noises; vacuum cleaners; police, ambulance, and fire engine sirens, or cars backfiring; loud music or television programs not of the child's choosing; public announcement systems and intercoms; people tapping, clicking, or snapping fingers or objects (such as a pencil); and people laughing, talking, or sneezing loudly.

Taste and Smell

Certain smells (especially food scents and perfumes or toiletries) and tastes may also be overwhelming. On occasion, a child may gag and vomit in reaction to the sensation of the smell or texture of foods. Unable to explain herself in the moment, the child may bolt from the environment if the smells or tastes become too much for her to handle.

Visual Sensitivity

Because many people with Asperger's are very visual in how they absorb and process information, they may also become readily overwhelmed by too many visual details in a single environment (think Wal*Mart on a Saturday afternoon). The number of moving, flapping, or spinning objects paired with the vivid mix of colors and combined with too many people cramped together in a single location can push the child with Asperger's into sensory overload. The same is true for many of us!

Light that is too intense can also cause pain and discomfort. Overhead fluorescent lighting is a harsh, abrasive, and unnatural illumination that is especially troublesome for many people with both Asperger's and autism. In addition to its intensity, fluorescent lighting may flicker and buzz. The flickering and buzzing may go completely unnoticed by others but will become unbearable for the child with heightened sensitivities.

Touch

Finally, the sensation of touch may be equally over-whelming for the child with Asperger's. Being hugged, patted on the head or back, or picked up—espe-cially unpredictably and without warning or permis-sion—may cause the child to cry, bite, or even hit. The challenge is that children, particularly small children, often tend to be hugged, patted, and picked up simply because they're adorable. The people doing the touch-ing are well intentioned but don't yet understand that the concept of respecting someone's personal space also applies to children.

The texture of certain clothing fabrics worn against one's skin may create extreme discomfort and physical irritation as well. This unpleasant sensation has been likened to one's flesh being rubbed raw with sandpaper. For some, cotton and natural fiber clothes are a must to ward against the manifestation of skin welts and rashes. Conversely, other children with Asperger's may welcome (and initiate seeking out) the sensory input provided by the deep-pressured touch offered by bear hugs and mas-sage, or burrowing under sofa cushions and mattresses, or self-swaddling in comforters and sleeping bags. The difference here is that these activities occur on the child's terms and at her specifications of endurance.

Other Commonalities

Another commonality children with Asperger's Syn-drome may have with those with autism is "flat affect" expressions and somewhat different speech patterns. A flat affect refers to facial expressions that are fixed or "artificial" in appearance instead of naturally animated. The child may not laugh or smile unless cued to do so in an appropriate situation, or the child may appear to have a collection of rehearsed or "canned" reactions to match certain circumstances.

The Way Your Child Speaks

The child's way of talking may also seem "flat" and monotone. The child's words may sound robotic and carefully measured. Or there may be a lilting tone to her voice, described by some as "singsong," in which her speech sounds like it's bouncing up and down when she talks.

Where's His Commonsense?

Often, the child with Asperger's may find it challenging to demonstrate or understand what others take for granted as a commonsense manner of thought. The child may have a logic all his own that perplexes or exasperates others because it is not representative of the norm. He may not grasp certain social rules or ways of doing things, explained away by others with the phrase "just because."

Keeping Order

It is also not uncommon for many children with Asperger's Syndrome to have a desire to maintain order, peace, and tranquility. Your child may (from his logic and perspective) initiate great and creative measures to make others happy and content to maintain the status quo, even if it means making decisions that adults may judge as unwise or unacceptable. It may have more to do with desiring to please in order to keep the peace than with being intuitive to others' needs.

It is important to appreciate that none of these reactions are typically "attention-seeking" or deliberately "bad" or noncompliant behaviors. They are a genuine reaction to extreme, hurtful disturbances in the child's immediate environment. For example, one mother assumed her son was engaging her in a power struggle when he refused to wear the new blue jeans he had picked out in the store and that she purchased for him. He complained that they scratched when he wore them. He was speaking truthfully, but mom wasn't listening carefully enough to his words. Washing the new jeans several times to soften them made them physically tolerable, and the conflict was resolved without further incident. This concept of distinguishing an "Asperger's moment" from typical kid behavior will make more sense as you continue reading. Helping the child with Asperger's to cope with his sensory sensitivities will be explored in more detail later in this book.

The *Diagnostic and Statistical Manual* does not presently include any of the previous autistic-like commonalities as clinical criteria for autism or Asperger's Syndrome. These attributes, while valid in many children, have become stereotypes when some doctors, journalists, and others generically describe those with Asperger's Syndrome. Asperger's is as unique and individual an experience as each individual is unique. You may find that some, all, or none of these nonclinical, autistic-like commonalities make sense when you think about your child's way of being in the world.

DOES THIS SOUND LIKE YOUR CHILD?

Your child may have Asperger's Syndrome if he or she finds it difficult to make friends; doesn't seem to understand nonverbal communications, like body language or facial expressions; doesn't understand or appears insensitive to others' feelings; is deeply passionate about one or more subject areas; is not physically graceful; has great difficulty accepting change in routine or schedule; or has a different or mechanical-sounding speech patterns.

Diagnosing Today

There has been a great deal of attention given by the media to the staggering, skyrocketing increase in the numbers of children identified with autism. It has been legitimately described as an epidemic explosion. Fifteen years ago, it was estimated that 1 in 10,000 individuals was autistic. In the 1990s, the estimate narrowed to 1 in 1,000, then 1 in every 500, then 1 in every 250 children. Today, the statistics fluctuate regularly, growing closer and closer all the time.

Recent tallies, such as that proffered by *Time* magazine in 2002, suggest that 1 in every 150 children under the age of ten has autism.

Why the Increase in Cases?

According to a 2002 study commissioned by the California Legislature, during the past fifteen years in the state of California alone, the number of children identified with autism has leapt by 643 percent. Another recent statistic estimated that 1 in every 5 children has either autism, dyslexia, attention deficit hyperactivity disorder, or some form of uncontrollable aggression. In 2003, the federal Centers for Disease Control and Prevention estimated that of the children born daily in the United States, 53 will be diagnosed with autism, or roughly 19,000 infants per year. As noted earlier, this rise is occurring without any single known cause or indicator.

How to Understand the New Findings

Where does this leave our understanding of the prevalence of Asperger's Syndrome? With so much attention being given to young children newly diagnosed with autism, those with Asperger's Syndrome are not usually identified and tracked in the same manner by doctors or our education system. We may speculate that there are a number of reasons for this:

- Families who live in isolated or rural areas, or have limited contact with others with similar-aged, typically developing children, may not recognize their child's differences or may be distanced from proper support systems to obtain a diagnosis.

- Family practitioners and other physicians may be unaccustomed to identifying the symptoms of autism, let alone understanding the criteria for Asperger's Syndrome. They may have little to no experience with Asperger's or limited resources from which to gather more information.

- The child of school age undiagnosed with Asperger's may be labeled as noncompliant or lazy. Parents and teachers may believe she is simply not applying herself to her full potential.

- The child may be seen as simply quirky or especially gifted, leading to the "Little Professor" moniker that has become a popular way of describing children with Asperger's who present as technically proficient miniature adults.

- The child may have a diagnosis of hyperlexia, an experience that may outwardly present itself as similar to Asperger's in that the child may be highly fluent. Hyperlexia is marked by a precocious capacity for reading that far exceeds the child's chronological age; however, the child may be unable to comprehend all that has been read. The child may be fascinated with numbers, may need to keep specific routines, and may be challenged in social interactions.

- The child has a "ballpark" diagnosis but, as noted earlier, it is labeled as PDD-NOS or high-functioning autism. As such, it is not specifically identified as Asperger's.

What about a Missed Diagnosis?

Because the clinical criteria for Asperger's calls for no significant cognitive or developmental delays, it is often undetected until a child is past the age of eligibility for early intervention services. It is also possible for Asperger's Syndrome to go undiagnosed altogether, because it can be so subtle. It could also be misdiagnosed as another issue such as a learning disorder, attention deficit disorder, attention deficit hyperactivity disorder, dyslexia, schizophrenia, generalized anxiety disorder, Tourette's syndrome, obsessive-compulsive disorder, oppositional defiant disorder, bipolar disorder, intermittent explosive disorder, or depression—all mental health experiences listed in the *DSM*.

What Is the Truth?

Given all this, what *do* we know about the prevalence of Asperger's Syndrome? Like autism, Asperger's knows no social, cultural, or economic boundaries. And, also like autism, it is four times more likely to be found in males than females (again, for reasons presently unknown). Until recently, Asperger's, like the prevalence of autism, was believed to be largely a male experience, but as our culture is becoming more aware and better educated to such social issues, more females with Asperger's are being identified. Conservative estimates conclude that 1 in every 1,000 children has Asperger's Syndrome. However, as we've seen with autism, the increasing recognition of Asperger's will surely prompt that statistic to increase in the near future.

Chapter 2

Evaluation and Diagnosis

10 Things You Will Learn in this Chapter

- If a formal diagnosis is right for your family.

- About how your child's behavior will differ from his/her peers.

- How to deal with family, friends, or neighbors who make comments about your child.

- Why you should consult different resources and not just the DSM.

- About the pros and cons of a formal diagnosis.

- What teens and adults with Asperger's say about diagnosing children.

- Which doctor(s) you should contact and when.

- How to prepare yourself and your child for the first appointment.

- How you can help the doctor to make the right diagnosis.

- About the Early Intervention Program and whether or not your child is eligible.

Is a Diagnosis Necessary?

Each family is unique and different. The relationships between spouses, children, and extended family can vary drastically. Some families are distant and disconnected from one another. It may be difficult for some family members to outwardly express love and caring. Other families are remarkably and consistently loving and resilient. Still others fall somewhere in between. The dynamics of your family will likely determine how you proceed in seeking a diagnosis of Asperger's Syndrome for your child.

Your decision to pursue a formal diagnosis is a personalized and individualized decision to make. There is no "correct" time to form this decision, although many parents agree that they wish to know their child's diagnosis definitively and as early in their child's development as possible.

Is Your Child Different?

In observing your child grow and learn, you may have noticed differences in how she is developing when compared with her peers. You may have noticed significant differences in how she interacts with other children. For instance, she may seem not to understand the social rules that other children seem to naturally abide by, such as taking turns in a game. She may play with her toys in ways that are unique but unintended for the toy's purpose, like dismantling the toy to more closely examine its moving parts. The way she talks may sound overly formal, such as addressing you and your spouse as "mother" and "father" instead of mommy and daddy, or inappropriately calling you by your full first name (i.e., "Oh Deirdre, please come help me with my bath now"). She may not be as physically graceful as you might wish for her. Or her temper may be prone to escalate when she loses control of her environment.

A BETTER PARENTING PRACTICE

Every family is unique, as are the dynamics and interplay of each family member's relationships with one another. In reflecting upon your child's different way of being, be mindful of not ascribing blame to yourself or others for having "caused" Asperger's Syndrome in your child. Remember, this was the basis of the now-archaic "Refrigerator Mother" theory.

When Others Say Something

Perhaps family, friends, or neighbors have brought some of these issues to your attention. They may wonder or worry if you've witnessed the same differences. When this occurs, it will be important to remember that these people are usually not being nosy, pushy, or humiliating for the sake of making you feel like an inadequate parent. Your concerned family, friends, or neighbors have good reasons for what they're doing, and they are doing the best they know how in the moment. They are merely trying to be helpful in drawing from their own life experiences or those of others they have known. Try listening to their communications and balancing the information they are sharing with what you know to be true.

You Know Best

As a parent, you know your child best. Is there a ring of truth in the collective observations of all? Are others confirming suspicions you've had but suppressed? If you see your child every day, the observations of the family member, friend, or neighbor who sees the child less frequently should be weighed carefully; your child's different way of being may be more apparent to them than to you. Conversely, if neither you nor your spouse is a stay-at-home parent, then you should accept the observations of your child care or day care professional with similar sincerity. The child care professional can offer you much valuable information about how your child spends his time during the day.

The Benefits of Knowing

Most likely, no one at this point will be in a position to suggest Asperger's Syndrome as a viable explanation of your child's way of being. So far, you have some questions and concerns about what you are seeing in your child. A place to start might be to compare what you know to be true of your child's development against the Diagnostic and Statistical Manual definition of Asperger's Syndrome. As you do so, please exercise caution. Specific symptoms in isolation of one another do not a syndrome make.

DID YOU KNOW?

Remember that the Diagnostic and Statistical Manual is a clinical document and is not intended to be family-friendly. If the prospect of researching the criteria for Asperger's Syndrome in the DSM feels a bit daunting, you may access the same or similar information through many of the Web sites listed at the back of this book. They are intended to be family- and individual-friendly.

Say your child has a particularly strong affection for watching the same video every day throughout the day and is interested in watching nothing other than this particular video. This may seem to fall under the category of intense preoccupation with an interest. But if you come up short in checking the remaining diagnostic criteria because your child demonstrates no other symptoms of Asperger's, then he simply has a very strong preference for that one video that may pass once he gets his fill of it.

Pros and Cons of a Formal Diagnosis

If you are discovering that the criteria for Asperger's might have application for your child, then you are faced with a decision about seeking a diagnosis. You may not wish to pursue a formal diagnosis at this time for one or more of the following reasons:

- You don't believe in labeling people's diversity.
- You'd rather wait to see if anything changes as your child continues developing.

- You don't feel that your child's differences are causing detriments in his life significant enough to obtain a diagnosis.
- You are scared or in denial of the situation.
- You are worried that your child will be stigmatized or singled out.

The benefits of obtaining a diagnosis may be:

- Putting a name and a framework to a collection of symptoms and traits instead of perceiving it all as your child's "bad behavior" or somehow your fault.
- Accessing a system of services and supports designed to give your child a head start in life as early as possible.
- Being able to educate family, friends, and neighbors about your child's unique way of being, when appropriate.
- Being able to educate your child in order to promote self-awareness and self-advocacy, as needed.
- Understanding and appreciating sooner your child's lifelong unique qualities, personal needs, and talents.

Adults with Asperger's Syndrome who were never diagnosed as children often ask, "Would it have been helpful to have had the diagnosis as a child?" We are still a long way from being effective in understanding Asperger's in a concerted, global sense, but having this knowledge early on in the lives of many adults might have aided them to:

- Experience greater success in school.
- Be better prepared for higher education, college, or trade school.
- Be better able to initiate and sustain relationships.
- Be better equipped to locate viable employment opportunities that best match skills and talents.
- Avoid struggles with mental health issues, or be better prepared to care for one's mental health.
- Be better prepared to avoid situations in which one may be unwittingly exploited.

Recently, a group of preteens with Asperger's was asked a question: "Is it helpful to know you have Asperger's?" They were unanimous in explaining that it was helpful and cleared up a lot of misperceptions and misinterpretations people had about why they do what they do.

Beginning the Process: Local Resources

If you determine that Asperger's Syndrome best describes your child's way of being and are interested in pursuing a diagnosis, your first course of action is to seek a referral to the appropriate clinician most qualified to make the diagnosis.

The best place to start is with your child's pediatrician. Your child's pediatrician may not in a position to make a formal Asperger's diagnosis, but can refer you to a specialist who can. You will need to inquire if he or she knows of a child psychiatrist, developmental pediatrician, and/or child psychologist who is experienced in seeing kids with autism spectrum differences, or Asperger's specifically. Hopefully your pediatrician can steer you in the right direction to getting a diagnosis for your child, whether it is Asperger's Syndrome or another condition.

Where You Live and Your Doctors

If you live in an urban area, there may be a multitude of doctors from which to select. You will need to narrow your range of choices. As autism has become commonplace, you may wish to begin by asking the pediatrician if he or she can tell you of any other patients who have been pleased with particular diagnosing physicians. The pediatrician may or may not be able to share this information based on client confidentiality or conflict of interest outside of a managed care physician's network.

If you live in a rural area, you should still ask your child's pediatrician for a referral, but there's a greater chance that the doctor may not know of anyone who specializes in making autism or Asperger's Syndrome diagnoses. Or, if the doctor does make a referral, depending upon your location you may have to travel a great distance to access a reputable and established medical center with a child psychiatry department, such as your nearest Children's Hospital.

Preparing for the Appointment

Once you make an appointment with a physician qualified to make an Asperger's diagnosis, it is important to be prepared. When setting up the appointment, ask the receptionist or nurse practitioner what kinds of information the doctor expects to receive from you. Is there a form or forms that may be faxed, e-mailed, or mailed to you in advance to save time and ensure a thorough and complete job? Be certain to clarify any insurance concerns you may have as well, and ask how the appointment will be billed. Ask for any information about in-office testing or assessment that may be conducted by the doctor. Is there anything you should be prepared for regarding those tests?

▶ A BETTER PARENTING PRACTICE

Preparing a psychiatric or psychological appointment for your child may be a very anxious time for you. Be careful of what your child overhears you saying to others. She may be acutely attuned to picking up on your frustrations and anxieties, which may impact her as well. Keep your phone contacts about this topic as private as possible.

Most often, the doctor will conduct an interview to ask specific questions designed to elicit information about your concerns. Depending upon your child's age, the doctor may wish to meet with your child alone to observe or interview her separately. Find out in advance if that is part of the process. Understand that, because of demand and client backlog, it may be several weeks before a qualified physician has room in his or her schedule to see you.

Of course, just as you are preparing for this appointment, you will need to help your child to prepare for it as well. Knowledge is power. Your child will do best if she feels safe and comfortable and in control. You may best accomplish this by:

- Explaining that the appointment is with a doctor who only asks questions and does not give shots or ask the child to engage in any other medical-type procedure.
- Sharing with your child your understanding of the structure and sequence of the appointment, including approximate wait time and duration.
- Sharing with your child whatever questions you expect the doctor to ask.
- Getting out a map to show the child exactly where your house is and the route you will take to the doctor's clinic. (Give the child the map or a photocopy and partner with her on driving directions while en route the day of the appointment.)
- Taking your child to the clinic ahead of time to familiarize her with the surroundings and to meet the doctor, if possible. (Take photographs to give to your child well in advance of the appointment.)
- Empowering the child to mark off the days until the appointment on a prominently displayed wall calendar.
- Allowing your child to bring a book or small toy related to her most passionate of interests

to defer the tedium of waiting before, during, and after the appointment. (The object of passion will also be a terrific icebreaker by which the doctor can initiate conversation with your child.)

These strategies should help you and your child feel fairly comfortable about the impending appointment.

The Doctor's Visit

During the appointment, it will be important for you to try to stay as focused as possible and to listen carefully to what the doctor is asking. Oftentimes during such a significant time, parents are filled with lots of nervous anxiety, some of which is completely natural. Your anxiety will not be helpful to the doctor if you go overboard. Don't bring stacks of your child's medical, educational, and other records to show the doctor well beyond anything that was requested. Don't digress into lengthy stories intended to highlight one incident in great detail. Be careful not to frequently interrupt in order to press your own agenda, such as pressuring the doctor to make an on-the-spot judgment call.

You Can Help

To be helpful to the doctor, bring exactly what was requested. If you bring additional information, only offer it if you think it's warranted or if it helps to illuminate a specific point. Accept that the doctor may not need it at that time. Be prepared to discuss why you believe your child might have Asperger's Syndrome.

Talk about specific clinical symptoms—not behaviors. Only tell concise stories that illustrate your rationale. When you talk about symptoms, you're talking the doctor's language. He or she will be far better equipped to discern a diagnosis if you are clear and brief in offering such information. Otherwise, the doctor must sort through a laundry list of descriptive "behaviors," trying to match what you're communicating against the *DSM* criteria. Allow the doctor to guide the interview, and interject with questions only as needed.

A BETTER PARENTING PRACTICE

By connecting with other parents—either locally, statewide, or nationally—by phone or e-mail, you may receive valuable information about the diagnostic process for your child. Experiences will vary from person to person, but you will surely obtain valuable "pointers" that may help you feel comfortable in knowing what's best to do and say.

It is unlikely that you will walk away from the appointment with an Asperger's Syndrome diagnosis. The doctor will need time to absorb and process all the information he or she has gathered from you. A written summary of the meeting and the doctor's observations and findings will be forthcoming. If several weeks go by and you don't receive such a report, contact the clinic to check on its status.

Observation and Intervention

There are other avenues to access information on Asperger's Syndrome or community services and supports. Every state's county government system has an office that serves infants and children, adolescents, and adults with a variety of different ways of being, covering autism, intellectual impairment, and mental health issues. (The same or neighboring office may address child welfare, domestic violence issues, and alcohol and substance abuse.) In some areas it is called the Office of Developmental Disabilities. In others, it is known as the county Mental Health–Mental Retardation Office—a title that has become antiquated and offensive (not to mention intimidating) to many parents. That is not to say that such office is in every county; two or more counties may share a hub office. The phone number for your county's local disabilities office is located in the blue pages of your phone directory.

The Early Intervention Program

If your child is younger than five years old, when you call the office, ask for a referral to the Early Intervention Program in order to arrange an assessment of need. Early Intervention is a federally mandated program delivered by every state free of cost to families of children with developmental delays from infancy to three years old. The Individuals with Disabilities Education Act (or IDEA) stipulates the provisions for delivery of early intervention. Children over age three who need early intervention services can be evaluated by their local school district, even if they aren't in school yet.

Eligibility

The Early Intervention Office will arrange to have someone come to your home at your convenience to assess your child for developmental delays. If your child qualifies for the program, he may be able to access a variety of professionals and therapists who will educate you about meeting his needs. The challenge in accessing Early Intervention for a child with Asperger's Syndrome is that Asperger's is so subtle that kids "fall through the cracks" and go undetected until they are much older than Early Intervention age. Additionally, according to the clinical criteria for Asperger's Syndrome, a child should demonstrate *no* cognitive or developmental delays. This would make a child ineligible for Early Intervention.

Your child may experience some physical fine- or gross-motor limitations that could make her eligible for the program, or the Early Intervention representative will support you in accessing any other local resources that may prove helpful. If your child is blind or deaf, she may also qualify for the program, but the services and supports offered will focus on your child's differences and will likely be unable to address Asperger's Syndrome.

However, one area of developmental delay identified for Early Intervention eligibility is social-emotional development, or how well a child relates to others. If your child's social differences are significant enough to cause you concern and she is within Early Intervention age, you may be able to access certain services and support designed to help engage her socially.

DID YOU KNOW?

Early Intervention is a family-centered program. The intent of the professionals involved is to work directly with you to accommodate your needs, address your concerns, arrange in-person contact according to your schedule, and link you to other people and opportunities that may prove helpful.

Help from School

Still, the symptoms of Asperger's Syndrome may go unnoticed until your child is of school age. If you have not been cognizant of your child's symptoms or you've been in a "let's wait and see" holding pattern, your child's educators may bring it to your attention. They may have noticed your child's distractibility, difficulty in understanding what is expected of him, seeming challenges in social connectedness, and other traits associated with Asperger's. They may recommend a consultation with the school psychologist, who may discuss Asperger's Syndrome with you.

Student Assistant Program

The school psychologist will usually be a member of a school team called the Student Assistance Program, or SAP. As a rule, most school psychologists don't make clinical diagnoses such as Asperger's Syndrome, but the psychologist can partner with you and the SAP team as part of an assessment process to identify more specific areas of need that interfere with your child's ability to learn.

A BETTER PARENTING PRACTICE

If your parental instinct is telling you that your child is struggling socially or academically and you think it is possibly due to Asperger's Syndrome, address it with your child's school professionals as soon as possible. Be clear, direct, and concise about what you are thinking, feeling, and seeing, and request their support.

The school psychologist may assist with observations of your child during the school day or make a referral to a clinician who can make a diagnosis. The school psychologist will then work with the doctor's report to aid the SAP team in supporting your child's social and emotional needs and in making accommodations for your child in the general education curriculum.

Now What? Self-Understanding

So the diagnosis has been made. Now what? Once you obtain an Asperger's Syndrome diagnosis for your child, you are faced with another significant hurdle: disclosure. With the advent of diagnosis, you will likely be required to interact with others—family, friends, neighbors, doctors, and educators—for the purpose of discussing the diagnosis. You will need to use discretion with disclosure. Please be mindful of being careless of when, how, and with whom you share information, especially if it occurs in your child's presence. Remember, we're talking about a child, and the child is not defined by the diagnosis. Always remember the concept of the self-fulfilling prophecy. If your child overhears you discussing the diagnosis more often than her gifts and talents and her amazing way of being in the world, she will likely become defined by the diagnosis exclusively. When you appear comfortable readily disclosing sensitive information, you model this behavior for others who think it perfectly acceptable or necessary. And so begins an otherwise avoidable downward, perpetual spiral.

Empower Your Child

As early as possible, empower your child as the keeper of information. As a parent, you will know best when, where, how, and under what circumstances you broach a discussion about Asperger's Syndrome with your child. As with any sensitive discussion, you will want to:

- Follow your child's lead by sharing as much or as little information as needed.
- Balance the discussion by highlighting everything you love about your child.
- Underscore that the diagnosis is just a name—nothing else has changed.
- Be prepared to answer any questions your child may have.
- Give your child the opportunity to write, draw, or otherwise make concrete the information as they envision it.
- Talk about disclosure as the concept of being choosy or very selective about when, where, and with whom personal information is shared.

Regardless of your child's age, he is now your partner in all matters of disclosure. This is the respectful response to supporting the child with Asperger's Syndrome. This means that *prior* to arbitrarily sharing personal information about your child's diagnosis, you check with him first to:

- Ask permission to disclose.
- Explain why you believe it is necessary.
- Be open to being flexible if he protests.
- Offer opportunity for compromise.
- Discuss the best, most gentle, most respectful way to disclose the information.

Chapter 3

Living With Asperger's Syndrome

10 Things You Will Learn in this Chapter

- How your child's diagnosis might teach you more about yourself or your spouse.
- What to do if you suspect that you or your spouse may have Asperger's too.
- About a website that puts emphasis on problem solving within marriages and relationships that are affected by Asperger's Syndrome.
- How a diagnosis can change your family dynamic.
- To work with your child to determine how much they want to disclose to family members, friends, teachers, and other people.
- How to explain to siblings and help them cope.
- How to deal with other people's inappropriate reactions to the news of your child's disorder.
- How to deal with public meltdowns and people's reactions to them.
- About how to educate others if you feel the desire to.
- Questions to ask yourself before you become overly frustrated or angry with your child.

Your Role in All of This

When you received your child's diagnosis, you probably endured a number of thoughts, feelings, and emotions. It may have been difficult to make sense of them at the time until you sorted them out and processed them through. As you learned more about Asperger's Syndrome, some of your thoughts might have begun to crystallize more clearly.

Among these thoughts may have been reflections of the diagnosis as it pertained to you and your own childhood, or that of your spouse. Were there times you endured growing up, or while attending school, that now have meaning? You may find that your child's diagnosis puts into perspective your experiences or makes sense of your spouse's quirks and idiosyncrasies. If your child's differences went unnoticed and undiagnosed until he was in his later childhood years, could it be because no one in your immediate family observed anything unusual about him? Was his way of being already firmly entrenched with your family's typical, ordinary, everyday-life way of being?

These are some of the thoughts you may be pondering, and they are not unusual. This chapter is a resource to mothers and fathers who are beginning to understand that their child comes by his Asperger's Syndrome honestly; that is, it may be a genetic reflection of his parents.

Could It Be Genetic?

As previously noted, little factual information is known about Asperger's Syndrome. For many, it is an invisible disability because it is so subtle it can go undetected. At present, statistics and other data are sparse, and we may speculate that there are any number of adults with Asperger's living and working in our communities that are undiagnosed. One recent theory hypothesizes that certain types of people with "Asperger-like" traits—smart but antisocial—attract one another, leading to such couples bearing children with the same traits, only magnified due to an overload of genes. Dr. Fred Volkmar, a child psychiatrist at Yale University, estimates that Asperger's correlates with a genetic component more apparent than even autism. Dr. Volkmar suggests that about one-third of fathers or brothers of children with Asperger's show signs of Asperger's themselves, and there also appear to be maternal connections as well. This information increases the likelihood that Asperger's may be present in your own family. Think about your child's lineage—are there, or were there, brilliant and creative but blatantly eccentric family members?

Is this a Helpful or Hurtful Realization?

Depending upon your personality and the strength of your coping skills, this may be either relieving or disturbing information to consider. If the diagnosis is given and received with a "gloom and doom" mentality, you may lapse into a period of guilt or self-punishment. You may find yourself unjustly bearing the brunt of blame induced by yourself or your spouse. Parents of children with autism do tend to reflect stress tied to anxiety and depression when compared with parents of typical children.

But remember, Asperger's is a naturally occurring experience and is no one's fault. Hopefully, this text will empower you to avoid believing negative Asperger's stereotypes in favor of focusing on the positives.

Confronting the Possibility

For Dr. Liane Holliday Willey, author of the book *Pretending to be Normal: Living with Asperger's Syndrome*, learning of her daughter's diagnosis was personally liberating because it wasn't until then that she realized she, too, had Asperger's. She defined the experience as reaching the end of a race to be normal. At long last, she embraced self-acceptance and was now in a position to articulate her sensitivities using the framework of Asperger's. Dr. Willey's journey was challenging but she was supported by a husband who walked beside her on the path to self-discovery. Regrettably, not all families handle the experience of recognizing Asperger's in themselves as well as this.

DID YOU KNOW?

There are those marriages that simply do not sustain well under real or perceived pressures of raising a child with a different way of being. Families of children with Asperger's Syndrome are no exception. Educate and inform yourself and your spouse early on. Connecting with other parents in similar situations can dispel stigmatizing myths and stereotypes.

Recognizing Traits in You or Your Spouse

If you find yourself suspecting that you or your spouse also has Asperger's Syndrome, please consider the following:

- Arm yourself with knowledge and gather as much information as you can from the Internet or the resources listed in this book.
- Broach the subject with your spouse by asking open-ended or leading questions that will provide opportunity for reflection, like, "Do you think our child gets her love of science from your side of the family?"
- Because you are both still assimilating your child's experience, allow yourself and your spouse time to process this new twist on the situation.
- The conversations you have about Asperger's in the family should build slowly and incrementally.
- Avoid guilt, blame, and finger-pointing accusations like, "It's all your fault our child is this way."
- Offer to explore and research Asperger's Syndrome with your spouse or to provide your spouse with whatever literature you've already gathered.
- Discuss marriage counseling or other professional supports in partnership with your spouse.

DID YOU KNOW?

Asperger's Syndrome Partners and Individuals Resources, Encouragement and Support, or ASPIRES, is a Web site for spouses and supporters of adults diagnosed (or believed to be) on the autism spectrum, with emphasis on problem solving within marriages and relationships. Check it out at: *www.aspires-relationships.com.*

Understanding Asperger's as a probability for you and your spouse will be a learning time for you both. It can create marital stress and turmoil, or it can be an opportunity to strengthen and enhance your marriage.

Family Dynamics and Sibling Issues

Some families are remarkably resilient. Through unconditional love, they are able to persevere and meet new challenges while remaining whole and intact. Others seriously struggle or fall apart, and still others fall somewhere in between. Just as your family dynamics determine how your marriage will fare as you understand the significance of Asperger's for you and your spouse, so will your family makeup also determine how your child's brothers and sisters receive the same information. In other words, your children will take their cues from you and your spouse; the attitudes and actions you model will be reflected in them. They will not only project the values about their sibling's differences within the family, they will demonstrate these beliefs in school, the community, and the world at large.

Setting a Positive Example

It is crucial that you work toward setting a positive tone when first presenting your child's Asperger's Syndrome to his brothers and sisters. It not only impacts the quality of your immediate family relationships, but it also impacts the ways in which *all* your children perceive all people with differences for the rest of their lives.

When you broach the topic of Asperger's Syndrome with your child's siblings, consider these points:

- Partner with your child about the issue of disclosure to agree upon how much or how little to reveal.
- Decide if it's best to share the information with each sibling in privacy or if it should be done with the family as a group.
- Begin by highlighting the ways in which we are all more alike than different.
- Discuss the gifts and talents of your other children first and then discuss those of your child with Asperger's.
- Emphasize Asperger's as a natural experience and dispel fears about it being a contagious disease or something that can suddenly happen to just anyone.
- Don't play the pity card—you want your kids to be kids and to maintain their typical relationships as brothers and sisters, not walk on eggshells.

- Don't put unfair or unrealistic expectations on your child's siblings about increased responsibilities or the burden of future care-taking.
- Do discuss the ways in which the entire family is going to strive toward being more sensitive to the needs of your child—needs previously unacknowledged or unrecognized.
- Talk about respecting your child's ownership of confidentiality, discretion, and disclosure.
- Allow for process time and questions.

Finding a balance in how you love all your children is a fine art for any parent. It may be tough for your other children to see the kind of time you may invest with your child with Asperger's and not feel jealous or envious. Wherever possible, try to engage all your children in any activities that can include them all. If your child with Asperger's is receiving special instruction from an educator or therapist, are there games and routines that your entire family can take on? This will work toward family bonding, patience, and tolerance, and it will make learning fun for your child with Asperger's. The more you treat your child's way of being as natural and "no big deal," the more your child's siblings will automatically pitch in, help out, and pick up the slack without thinking or complaining beyond typical sibling bickering. The terrific ripple effect from this will be in how your children will grow to value diversity in all people.

Helping Siblings Cope

Still, there will be occasions when your child's siblings require your solid parental support when they are unable to manage or self-regulate internal or external pressures. Some pitfalls to be mindful of in observing your child's siblings may include coping with:

- Manifestation of mental health issues due to the stress (self-imposed or imposed by you), especially in older daughters who may develop depression or an eating disorder
- Perceived embarrassment caused by their sibling's way of being, especially in public
- Being ostracized by peers who don't want to hang around them or come over to your house because of your child with Asperger's
- Feeling perpetually pressured to "parent" or protect their sibling with Asperger's
- Becoming weary and worn out from constantly defending their sibling
- Feeling guilty when they want to go places and do things alone
- Feeling pressured by peers to reject their sibling

Hopefully, none of these areas will manifest as concerns because you and your family have, from day one of the Asperger's diagnosis, set a positive, inclusive tone in relation to each family member's place in the home, school, and community. But if you should recognize problems in any of these areas, it will be important to have a private "pow-wow" with your child's siblings to offer your love, praise, and reassurances.

DOES THIS SOUND LIKE YOUR CHILD?

As your child's brothers and sisters grow and mature, their sibling relationships can become strained. They may take on other interests and broaden their circle of friends and as a result, the child with Asperger's (who may remain static despite ongoing change) is left out. Remember that change can be very difficult and saddening for your child and he may require you to facilitate scheduled "family" or "sibling" time to help him cope.

Are there ways that you can compensate in partnership with your other children, especially if they've been feeling left out? Parenting is never set in stone; it changes from moment to moment. Be willing to admit it's true if you've inadvertently been neglectful. Plan some quality time with your child's siblings apart from the rest of the family. It may be rejuvenating for you all.

Should You Share What You Know?

Revealing your child's Asperger's Syndrome diagnosis to extended family members is an issue of disclosure. Sharing such information should occur in partnership with your child in order to determine how much or how little others need to know.

Do They Need to Know?

In weighing your decision, please consider the following:

- How often do you see these relatives?
- If you only see them once or twice a year, is it necessary to say anything?
- Can you foresee their reactions?
- If there's potential for gross misunderstanding, how will you handle that?
- If they are intrigued and interested, how will you handle that without breaching your child's trust about disclosure (sharing more than what you agreed upon)?
- Can extended family be entrusted to honor disclosure?
- Can they treat the subject with sensitivity and respect?

In the long run, the pros may outweigh the cons, and you and your child may decide it's simply no one's business at present. So many children with Asperger's can artfully "pass" and blend for the duration of a day with family that any differences may go completely unnoticed given all the other distractions. (Is it possible that your child comes across as downright complacent when compared to some of the more flamboyant children and adults at some of those gatherings?)

Prepare for Their Reactions

If you decide it is appropriate to disclose information about your child's diagnosis, you may need to be prepared to deal with the potential for extended family to show their ignorance (not a bad thing if they're open to education), overcompensation, or discomfort. You will need to consider how best to quell any situations that may arise from overreactions should your extended family express their concern about the entire family being stigmatized by the diagnosis. They may openly express hopelessness for your child's way of being, deluge you with literature that focuses on cures or "quick fixes," or, worse yet, confuse Asperger's Syndrome with autism or some other diagnosis. Passive-aggressive behavior may transpire if extended family members become increasingly distant due to their own issues in processing the information, or only want to spend time with your other children. The worst-case scenario may be if they exclude or uninvite you and your child from future family get-togethers. A better scenario might be if they are overly cautious—trying not to do or say the wrong thing. In the latter situation, there is, at least, a way to offer assurances and education.

Stay Aware and Be there to Help

Hopefully, your wisdom and savvy as a parent who is fast learning to be a strong and knowledgeable advocate will be of good service to you in setting the proper tone of sensitivity, respect, and unconditional love where extended family is concerned. In any case, to aid your child in surviving a day or more with extended family, you will wish to arm her with ammunition in the form of self-advocacy and coping skills prior to attending family gatherings.

A BETTER PARENTING PRACTICE

You may be approached by family, friends, and relatives who genuinely desire to learn more about Asperger's Syndrome. Hear them out and allow your intuition to guide you in how much you wish to be their single "point of contact" where all things Asperger's are concerned. You may want to let them borrow this book for starters or refer them to specific Web sites that you found of good service.

Agree upon the time duration of being there (and *stick to it!*), and ensure that your child has some materials related to her passion to quietly indulge in if she feels overwhelmed. Also be certain to locate an area where your child can retreat, undisturbed by others, to recuperate during much needed "downtime." Show her where it is and assure her that she may use it at will. Check with your family in advance to find out what materials your child may access with their permission. Then, make sure your child knows where books, TV or videos, crayons, pen or paper, and Internet access can be found for solitary downtime activities. Other strategies that will be of enormous benefit in such situations will be discussed in detail later on in this book.

Your Child's Place in the Community

Sharing information about your child with neighbors, acquaintances, or total strangers in your community is no different than the process of determining when, where, and how to share the same information with family. Weigh carefully the drawbacks and positives that may come from sharing this information. It is an issue of disclosure that you should discus in advance with your child in order to be as considerate and respectful of his feelings as possible. As before, ideally, your child should be encouraged to be his own advocate as early as possible in order to decide how much or how little to tell others about his way of being, if it's even necessary at all.

Watch How You React

Some parents find themselves exasperated and embarrassed by their child's public meltdowns. They may garner stares, raised eyebrows, whispers, or flat-out denouncements of "Why can't you control your child?!" There are those who decide to forego discretion and bluntly address gawking onlookers by revealing there child's diagnosis right there, on the spot. They may pass out "For Your Information" business-size cards that state, "My child has Asperger's Syndrome and this is what you might see," followed by a list of meltdown behaviors or behaviors others may find quite peculiar. The mother of one young girl explained her daughter's prolonged staring at a neighbor-lady exclusively in terms of her Asperger's Syndrome.

"This Is Asperger's"

You may find yourself in the position of these parents who want to educate others and simply want a little patience and understanding in the moment. But are you best serving your child by revealing such intimate information, or are you fueling misperceptions and stereotypes—especially if you explain "This is Asperger's Syndrome"—at the height of your child's public meltdown? Aren't you, in effect, sending a message to the community that "This is what Asperger's Syndrome *looks* like"? You know Asperger's Syndrome encompasses many things, and your child's inability to endure certain environmental stimuli is but one sliver of who he is as a human being. Think of the impressions people take away with them after being told, "This is Asperger's Syndrome." Would you want to be regarded in this way when you know you aren't at your best and you're coping the best way you know how?

Ask Yourself . . .

As one mom asked, "Isn't it okay to express your anger, upset, and disappointment to your child for the way she behaved?" We're all human and as the parent of a child with a different way of being, nerves will fray and are bound to wear thin. In these times, you would vent your frustration to *any* of your children. Bottom line is, parents can "lose" it from time to time, but before expressing your extreme dissatisfaction with your child's conduct, ask yourself:

- Am I being fair?
- Am I making this an issue about Asperger's?
- Am I disclosing information publicly out of anger?
- Have I been clear in giving my child concrete, visual information in advance about my expectations?

If you believe you've been fair, then remember to focus on addressing your child's behavior in the community as inappropriate to the environment, instead of making it about Asperger's Syndrome. The mom who "outed" her daughter when she stared at a woman too long had the best solution of all. She decided that, next time, she would simply point out that her daughter appreciated the diversity of people's faces, jewelry, and clothing. She may be surprised at the way her positive "spin" creates an opportunity for relationship building.

Chapter 4

Your Child's Ability to Develop Relationships

10 Things You Will Learn in this Chapter

- An analogy that helps explain how your child makes friends.
- To help your child form bonds
- How deconstructing your child's favorite song can teach him/her about friendship.
- How using visual aids, like cartoon drawings, can help children learn about their peers.
- To teach your child good conversation starters and enders that will aid him/her in conversation.
- Phrases your child can use to keep up with quick conversations.
- About classes, events, and programs that will help your child become part of the community.
- How finding good allies will help your child grow and develop into a successful adult.
- About the right balance of work and play time—and how it's different when it comes to your child.
- Why he/she desires to be alone.

How Your Child Interacts

When you consider your child as an individual with Asperger's Syndrome, how does he fare in social conversation? Some children may appear shy and withdrawn, rarely speaking unless spoken to. Others may dominate the conversation with lengthy discussions about their most passionate interests. Your child may reflect these traits at different times, or fall somewhere in between. The social interaction skills you instill in your child now will have long-term benefit as he matures through adolescence and into adulthood. Learning how to develop social circles and relationships that can lead to friendship is important to your child's future successes and mental health stability.

The child who appears shy and withdrawn likely wants to feel welcomed and included by others but doesn't know where to begin. Similarly, the child who releases the equivalent of a verbal dissertation knows how to talk circles around that topic and may think that everyone has the same degree of interest such that they are spellbound. This child also doesn't realize the mechanics of social conversation.

Friendship Is a Dance

As metaphors and analogies help to enhance our understanding, consider that, in both instances, each child wishes to partake in the "Dance of Reciprocal Flow" (not to be confused with "The Electric Slide"). The first child is partnerless, awaiting an invitation to the dance. When the invitation doesn't come, she may feel hopeless. She may internalize these feelings, frustrated by not understanding others or herself. This may lead to a sense of guilt or blame, which could fuel depression. The second child has leaped into the dance without first having learned the steps. He, too, is partnerless but believes that all those present are his exclusive dance partners, available to him at any given moment. Both children are set up to be singled out for their differences and potentially stigmatized for not knowing the dance that most everyone else was born knowing, or absorbed simply by growing up neurotypical.

Learning the Dance

Developing friendships means either learning the Dance of Reciprocal Flow (and some are more masterful dancers than others), or approximating it well enough such that one blends nearly seamlessly for the time spent on the dance floor. It is a gradual process. Not one of us masters the dance immediately; we improve and gain more confidence as we practice the dance steps. As you've learned, most children with Asperger's Syndrome assimilate information in ways that are concrete and visual.

As your child's instructor in the Dance of Reciprocal Flow, you will wish to map this out for her, similar to the way that some people learn to dance by following the black, silhouetted footprints positioned on the floor. As they memorize the dance routine and position of each step, they make fewer and fewer missteps. The dance becomes more fluid, requiring less effort and less thought. Finally, the footprint outlines fade altogether. They are now visible only in one's consciousness, unseen by others. Some will require intermittent, periodic "polishing" to brush up on the dance steps; others will retain it always, permanently etched in their minds. The importance in learning the dance is to know when and where to buoy your partner so that you both work together to create one whole presentation.

Different Teachers and Individual Styles

A challenge is that, while everyone dances the dance, we've all had different instructors or role models. As such, we approach the dance with our unique, individual style and flair, reflective of our personality. Some of us may even improvise and break the rules, like those with a penchant for interrupting conversation or talking with their mouth full of food or gum. These nuances make discerning appropriate conversational flow difficult, but it really is a matter of etiquette. Your child should never be faulted for being polite during conversation, even if it sounds a bit "stiff" or formal.

Using Music to Teach

To poise your child for developing friends, you will wish to explain the Dance of Reciprocal Flow using a similar analogy—unless your child is passionate about dancing and would relate well. Another analogy that might be helpful in your child's understanding may include deconstructing your child's favorite song. Music can be extremely important to kids with Asperger's, and all music is based upon the principle of call and response. According to the song's composition, there is a time when one sings or plays an instrument; this is the "call." Then there are times to pause and remain silent in order to await the "response." It is similar to the way in which two-way conversation is supposed to work.

To solidify this concept, you will want to draw this with your child while you start and stop the song. Help your child identify one singer or one instrument and represent that on paper. Your child may even wish to use different colors to differentiate the participants in the song. Break the song down into portions and support your child to understand how all the pieces flow through call and response. In the most basic example, think of "Frère Jacques." If sung in "round robin" style, the song begins with the initial call being echoed in a response as additional communication partners are gradually added in.

Using Cartoon Characters to Teach

Your child may respond well to understanding social conversation when her favorite TV cartoon characters are involved. Again, it will be best if you are in a position to start and stop the action in order to highlight good and inappropriate conversation styles.

DOES THIS SOUND LIKE YOUR CHILD?

Visuals are very useful survival tools in learning for many children with Asperger's Syndrome. Your child may already enjoy drawing or creating computer art now. Often, kids fabricate elaborate characters and complex plots and scenarios. It might be good sense to build upon that when mapping or reviewing social interactions between real-life people known by you and your child.

More Helpful Tools

Help your child to reinforce what she's just seen by drawing it out on paper. Suggest that you both modify the conversation a bit. It may be a good, objective opportunity to demystify a real-time social interaction that failed your child. Using cartoon characters to take on a similar situation is a nonthreatening way for your child to deconstruct the issues. When finished, you may ask, "Isn't this like what happened with you and Leslie last Saturday?" Next, discuss ways your child might approach the situation differently if similar circumstances arise.

Other useful analogies to conversation may include observing how animals interact and envisioning their "voices," or using the concept of maps where streets and highways converge and intersect. As always, maximize the benefit by using words and pictures, reviewing the information routinely until it is no longer needed.

Practicing Conversations

Another way to get to know others with the goal of making friends is to have a "bag of tricks," consisting of Conversation Starters and Enders. Developing a repertoire of such tricks or skills will be of lifelong good service. Many children with Asperger's have terrific rote memories if they are able to create images of situations to best "match" the Conversation Starter or Ender. To begin, partner with your child to break down, in writing and pictures, lists for each area. Here are a few sample Conversation Starters:

- Greetings like "What's up?" "How's it going?" or "Hey" are fine for interacting with typical peers.
- More respectful greetings for teachers and other adults may include, "Good morning/afternoon, Mr. Eschelman," or simply, "Hello" or "Hi."
- "What did you do over the weekend?"
- "What did you watch on TV last night?"
- "What are you doing after school?"

Sample Conversation Enders may include:

- "I gotta go now."
- "I'll catch (or see, or talk to) you later."
- "Take it easy."
- "See you tomorrow (or tonight, or Monday)."

With your child, try coming up with additions to the list. What do favorite cartoon or TV characters use as Conversation Starters or Enders that are socially acceptable and fit well on these lists? Talk about how no one "owns" these Conversation Starters or Enders; anyone can use them. Your child will need to be prepared for what comes next should he not initiate a Starter or Ender.

Feedbacks and "Slip-Ins"

Next, discuss and map out lists for Conversation Feedbacks and Conversation "Slip-Ins." Conversation Feedbacks are responses to Conversation Starters or Enders initiated by someone else. Conversation Feedbacks may include responding with a question in order to elicit more information from the other person. Think of it like constructing a building or a model of some structure. Each piece of the conversation can add layers to the foundation either person began. When conversation changes topic, the process should begin anew—even if the building is uncompleted.

Still, there may be times when we don't know how to respond and a simple, affirming interjection will indicate that we're at least listening. Conversation Feedbacks are always useful tools to "fall back on" whenever one is uncertain of what to say and may include phrases such as:

- "I don't know what that is; tell me more."
- "I never heard of that before; can you explain it better to me?"
- "That's really neat!" or "That's interesting!"
- "Cool!" or "Awesome!"
- "I'm sorry about that."

Conversation Slip-Ins are socially acceptable alternatives to interrupting conversation. Your child will need to appreciate, through words and images, that it is considered rude to interrupt in conversation, but there are ways to "slip in" without being rude. You and your child will wish to identify when this works best (usually during a conversation lull or when someone has stopped talking). Conversation Slip-Ins may include:

- "Is it okay if I say something now?"
- "Excuse me, please."
- "May I add to what you're saying?"

- "Pardon me for interrupting." (formal or professional setting)

Some of these might be too formal for a child and would better suit a young adult. Perhaps you and your child can come up with others to add to this list. Once all the lists are in writing with images (or keyed into the computer), your child will be in a better position to practice these strategies in real-time situations. If you are very familiar with how you have both formatted or coded the information into imagery, you can support your child by discretely coaching her to call up the proper analogy suited to the moment. (For example, "Remember, this is just like when Daphne told Scooby Doo, 'Take it easy.'") Mistakes and unexpected circumstances are bound to arise, and these will require private and respectful debriefing to explain. With time, you and your child can modify and adapt his bag of tricks to become adept in the Dance of Reciprocal Flow.

Chances to Bond

There is no guarantee that understanding how conversation flows will lead to friendships. As previously discussed, building upon your child's most passionate interests and connecting to others with the same, or similar, passions will usually foster a depth to the relationship beyond mere surface conversation. Where your child may need you is in fostering situations in which she can meet others who are as equally impassioned. Once connected with at least one other peer who "gets" her and speaks the same language, your child will feel terrific. Knowing that others value what she has to offer will bolster her self-esteem. There is no better way to feel bonded with others than through mutual love of something or someone.

Finding Opportunities

What opportunities are available in your community by which you can support your child in making contacts to build upon his passion for insects, astronomy, Japanese animation, or other topics? If you are uncertain, start by pursuing the following:

- Programs and special events offered by your local library.
- Community projects or special celebration days.
- Opportunities offered through the newspaper, local circulars, or "merchandiser" type papers.
- Opportunities offered through local television and radio stations.
- Community classes such as arts and crafts, or martial arts.
- After-school activities sponsored in your district.
- Programs and special events offered by your local historical society or museums.
- Special events sponsored by local athletic leagues.

You may find other venues in your community to add to this list. As noted before, one of the most powerful and advantageous ways to connect with others with similar passions is through the Internet. The possibilities are endless.

A BETTER PARENTING PRACTICE

Your child's use of the Internet should be determined by the same rules and cautions you'd set for any of your children, but communication with others by e-mail or instant messaging is social and it should be valued as such.

Your child may learn more about other kids of the same age, beyond just the passion they share, by locating them on a map and learning about the local industry, economy, and more. The child passionate about Japanese animation may even have the chance to communicate with someone of that culture. They can compare notes and exchange ideas about the video games each is developing.

Social "Practice" Groups

In some communities, parents and professionals have banded together to form meeting groups for kids with Asperger's Syndrome. These gatherings provide a forum for unconditional acceptance in a safe and comfortable environment. Such groups do not advocate exclusion from typical children; rather, they are an opportunity for some children to learn social skills in a place where it's perfectly acceptable to mess up as you learn and practice.

One such social group for kids was initiated in Cherry Hill, New Jersey, in the spring of 2003. The Friendship Club was begun by a group of interested parents wanting activities and resources for their children with Asperger's. The program is sponsored through the Jewish Family and Children's Service of Southern New Jersey and staffed by parents, educators, and therapists.

The group meets weekly, teaching socially accepted rules and skills through role-playing games and worksheets. The lessons may involve comprehending that it's okay to make mistakes, dealing with teasing from others, or learning how to take "no" for an answer without melting down. The Friendship Club also emphasizes practicing eye contact and turn taking in conversation. Visibly posted rules and goals aid the children in staying focused when they require visual reminders.

In Your Neighborhood

Your local school district or county human service program may be able to tell you if any such meeting group already exists in your town or a neighboring town. If there is no such gathering group in your community, you may wish to consider establishing something similar in your area. Most likely, parents, previously unconnected, will want to meet in person to discuss the similarities of their lives; but the focus in this instance will need to be on supporting the children to meet their individual needs in a comfortable atmosphere.

Finding Allies

When your child becomes an independent adult, you want him to know how to surround himself with good, honest, and trustworthy people who will be kind and understanding of his different way of being. Such folks will be there for your child (and vice versa) unconditionally to aid him in navigating real life when he needs it. Professionals in your child's life may come and go. An ally is someone not paid to be a participant in your child's life and who is there for the long haul. Empowering your child to identify the qualities that make a strong, reliable ally is paramount.

DOES THIS SOUND LIKE YOUR CHILD?

Your child's closest allies should be immediately apparent to you. They are those persons to whom she naturally gravitates and who welcome her unconditionally. Can you accept that, despite being a parent, you may not be considered by your child to be an ally? Allies should be natural—not forced—relationships in order for them to endure.

Allies may include siblings (without external, parental pressure to be caregivers), extended family, neighbors, friends, members of the clergy, and others. An ally may even be someone in a romantic context; the person in your child's young adult or adult life that becomes his partner or spouse. Of course, there are no guarantees that an ally will remain a permanent fixture—people move, change jobs, divorce, or drift apart. But ally relationships tend to be long-standing personal investments.

Good Ally Examples

Allies can serve as friends, confidantes, and advocates. Sam's next-door neighbor in the movie *I am Sam* is a good example of an ally—someone who takes a strong personal interest in seeing an individual succeed despite his differences. Sam's neighbor is an older woman who is accessible to him when he needs her, especially for tips in raising his baby. The relationship is not one-sided, however, and the woman derives great pleasure from watching Sam grow and learn about life as a parent.

The qualities found in long term-allies may include someone who:

- Accepts your child just as she is.
- Is patient, sensitive, and loving.
- Makes the time to be present with your child.
- Returns phone calls and e-mails promptly and reliably.
- Is interested and intrigued by your child's passions.
- Is willing to apply his or her own life experiences and expertise to the relationship with your child.
- Believes your child is a beautiful, gifted human being with lots to offer the world.

Some kids with Asperger's relate better to adults. Because your child may portray herself as adultlike in her use of conversational language and interests, she may be treated as an equal and indulged by other adults. Your child may already have a strong rapport with one or more of your adult friends. This is okay—relationships are relationships; don't knock it. While you and your child continue to seek opportunities to connect with same-age peers, do not discourage your child from developing relationships with adults (unless you suspect their motives to be impure, which is likely not the case). If you seek to squelch those relationships simply because of age differences, it could be devastating to your child. Weigh your child's relationships with adults with your comfort level and allow your intuitions to guide you.

Free Time, Alone Time—What's Normal?

It is a stereotype that people with Asperger's Syndrome want to live solitary lives and deliberately isolate themselves from society in hermitlike existence. As more children are recognized to have Asperger's, there is a broadening awareness of the diversity among all people.

A BETTER PARENTING PRACTICE

Many of us cope with everyday stressors by indulging in our own personal relaxation techniques and routines, free from the demands of others. You may consider it "my time." Some people exercise, soak in a hot tub, read, or watch TV. We are all more alike than different, yet oftentimes parents and professionals place demands upon children as soon as they come through the door from school.

Remember the phrase "inherently gentle and exquisitely sensitive"? When one is bombarded daily by sensory stimuli that is irritating or hurtful, or when one is challenged to decipher the logic and rationale of others, it can become physically, mentally, and emotionally exhausting. We all relish our downtime—those fleeting opportunities when we can change into comfortable clothes, relax, and reward ourselves for having made it through another day. The child with Asperger's is no different, but his desire to be alone can be perceived as "abnormal" simply because the clinical diagnosis says so.

Make Time for Free Time

As a parent, you will wish to set rules for all your children about free time versus time you expect chores and homework to be accomplished. It is likely that your child with Asperger's loves nothing more than becoming deeply absorbed in his most passionate of interests—reading, drawing, Internet surfing, or watching TV. Ask that he abide by the rules you have agreed on, but don't penalize him for losing track of time unless you have just cause to believe it is deliberate. Be cautious of imposing your own biases about how "long is too long" to spend alone.

You may also have expectations about what being "social" should look like. But "social" should be defined differently for each individual, depending on that person's needs. You may value many friends as a mark of being socially successful. Some people with Asperger's are content with just a very few, select friends. Many are not social butterflies, don't wish to be, and never will be. Unless they wish to endeavor to become more social, such individuals may simply be the kind of folks who are completely comfortable with a small group of close-knit people. As a parent, you can arrange to expose your child to a variety of people within a range of environments and circumstances. Your child will guide you to those with whom she feels connected and wishes to know better.

Chapter 5

Your Discipline Challenges

10 Things You Will Learn in this Chapter

- How disciplining a child with Asperger's differs from disciplining other children.

- How "common sense" is different for you and your child.

- Effective ways to set rules and stick to them.

- Why you should be careful not to jump to conclusions and react prematurely.

- How making a list of rules and consequences may help you get on the same page with your child.

- Which types of discipline work best and why.

- When it's the right time to back off and when it's time to put your foot down.

- About the problems associated with being overprotective.

- About the three meltdown trigger areas—communication, pain and discomfort, and mental health issues.

- How to recognize meltdown triggers and avoid them.

Identify Your Approach

All parents are faced with the task of childrearing to the best of their ability. Loving your child as you do, you want to know you're doing the right thing. Because each child is a unique individual, there is no single method for raising your specific child, only sound generalizations for you to test and apply. Your approach to disciplining your child will likely draw from several things, including your memories of how you were disciplined as a child, strategies, philosophies, and ideas you've read and with which you concur, and personal observations of how your family, friends, and neighbors discipline their own children.

The key to disciplining your child with Asperger's Syndrome is to—first and foremost—remember these positive philosophies:

- Your child has good reasons for doing what he's doing.
- He's doing the very best he knows how to in the moment (and with what he's got available to him).
- He needs to feel safe and comfortable and in control.
- He will become unhinged by anything significantly un-predictable.
- Like most children, he won't respond to spanking or other corporal punishment.

Your child's need to feel in control should not be taken to extremes. Parents must set limits and expectations for all children. Having Asperger's Syndrome does not give one free reign to be out of control, and that should not be endorsed or indulged by you; you wouldn't allow any of your other children to do everything they want, whenever they please.

DID YOU KNOW?

Some parents of kids with Asperger's are accused of being too "soft" with their children. You know your child best. He may be a very sensitive individual, but you have the right as a parent to set realistic expectations of obligations and responsibilities the same as you would for any other child.

Before you scold, however, you will also need to be mindful that your child's logic will not necessarily reflect your idea of common sense. For example, imagine a teenager who is driving down the highway and sees a box in the middle of the road. He decides the box must be empty and drives over it, rather than around it. The box isn't empty and damages his car. Even though his logic is questionable, he did not deliberately attempt to damage the car.

Set Rules and Stick to Them!

Many parents "fly by the seat of their pants" in setting rules. That is, they assume a child should understand appropriate social behavior under a wide variety of specific circumstances and, when that doesn't occur, they scold in the moment.

For example, suppose you are in attendance at a wedding and your child with Asperger's is bored or distracted. To your chagrin, she insists on telling everyone around her the flight schedule of every major airline departing from your local airport in a loud, clear voice that carries. Your first reaction may be to "shush" her into silence. When that proves ineffective, you may firmly whisper to her to stop. When that doesn't work, you may take hold of her and make a threat, such as the loss of a reward, special privilege, or favored plaything. As a last resort, you may physically remove her from the setting. You have intervened when the situation required it.

Prevention before a Problem

As the parent of a child with Asperger's Syndrome, your approach to discipline should be one of *prevention,* not intervention. After we review steps to ensure prevention, we will revisit this exact scenario.

A BETTER PARENTING PRACTICE

Being the parent of a child with Asperger's Syndrome may draw upon all your sleuthing skills in discerning the truth when it comes to discipline. Don't be deceived by first impressions of a situation by readily jumping to the conclusion that your child has made a serious error in judgment. Give her time to explain. Was her motive altruistic (though way off base) or was she trying to protect someone else?

Your child with Asperger's Syndrome can only know what he knows. Many children with Asperger's interpret information in ways that are very literal and concrete. Remember Tom Hanks as the boy in a man's body in the movie *Big*? At a reception, he drew stares and raised eyebrows by attempting to eat the miniature corn as he would regular corn on the cob. He wasn't trying to be socially inappropriate on purpose. Never having had experience with the social conventions of consuming the mini hors d'oeuvres, he was doing his best in the moment.

Like the parent in the wedding scenario, you may expect your child to automatically "read" your body language and facial expressions of displeasure or to transfer what he's learned in a similar environment to the present situation. It doesn't usually work that way. Most importantly, your child is not consistently misbehaving solely for the sake of "being bad."

What to Expect—Communication Trouble

In all matters of disciplining the child with Asperger's Syndrome, you have the responsibility to be fair in how you communicate rules and expectations. Because your child will be most open to receiving this information in ways that are literal and concrete, this means making it tangible. That is, put it in writing as a simple, bullet-point list. It may even be a partnered agreement that you both review and sign together. This will provide your child with a personal investment in the agreement and give him an incentive to comply. The list of rules becomes your child's property and, depending upon the situation, should be kept in her pocket for ready reference. Be open and flexible enough to listen to her questions. Do not feel personally challenged, or that your child is trying to "outsmart" you. She is merely being direct in asking for clarification of what you're trying to communicate.

DOES THIS SOUND LIKE YOUR CHILD?

The ability to "call up" visual information at will does not necessarily mean your child can do this at your command. This may be confusing because he may recite, on cue, intricate details relative to his most passionate interests but be unable to "replay" concepts you've impressed upon him. Like all kids, your child may need visual reminders and practice to get it down.

Numbering each item on the list may aid your child's recall. You may even wish to decide, in partnership with your child, how many warnings she'll get to stop breaking the rules before you implement your standard means of discipline. This is fair. Now if we revisit the wedding scenario, both you *and* your child are well prepared with regard to your expectations (and those dictated by the environment) prior to going into the situation. Not only is this fair, it is prevention not intervention.

A sample list of rules for the wedding scenario might look like this:

Rules for Going to a Wedding

1. Before the service begins, it is okay to talk with other people, especially people I know.

2. When everyone is sitting down, people will usually be very quiet or whisper. Everyone expects me to be quiet or to whisper, too.

3. If I am not being quiet or if I am whispering too much, Mom or Dad (or spouse) will tell me about it and ask me to stop. They will do this because I am distracting other people who want to see and hear the service.

4. If I get bored during the service, I will think about something else, quietly draw or read, or play a silent game I bring with me.

5. When the service ends and people get up, it is okay to talk in my normal voice again.

When preparing to leave for the wedding, remind your child to bring the rules along (unless she is able to use photographic memory and recite them by rote). On the drive there, review the rules together. When you notice your child becoming restless during the service, she may need reminders about the alternatives you both agreed to. If your child requires a warning, be remindful of the rules and *why* she's getting the warning. You can generalize this positive strategy to numerous and similar social circumstances.

If your child continues to behave improperly, it may be appropriate to discipline at this time. The operative word here is "may," and to further complicate things, there might be mitigating factors to dissuade you from discipline in the moment. These factors will be discussed at the end of this chapter.

In Your Child's Eyes

Again, never assume your child will automatically transfer and apply information previously learned in one environment to a new situation that, in your mind, is remarkably similar. For that child, a new situation is a new situation.

Consider this example: A teenage boy with Asperger's once decided to drive his family's car while his parents were out. His family was preparing to junk the car and had let the insurance on it expire. The young man knew this but took the car out anyway. He believed the worst that might happen would be getting into a minor fender-bender and being held responsible for paying the damage costs, as had been his previous experience with car accidents. When he arrived home, his very upset parents confronted him. They were distraught over the implications of driving without insurance—the potential for a major collision that could've involved serious damage, injury, or death to others and for which they would be held personally responsible. The teenager had no idea of these potential ramifications of his actions. If he had, he likely would not have entertained the notion of taking the car anywhere.

Your Emotional Child

As previously acknowledged, your child with Asperger's Syndrome is likely to be very emotionally sensitive. She may tear up and weep at song lyrics or commercials.

He may be unable to keep from dwelling on a particularly disturbing news story. Given this, it's important that you never make idle threats in anger or exasperation that have finality to their tone, such as, "I wish you'd just disappear!" "I'm going to call the police to come get you!" or "I'm going to send you far away from here!"

We are all human, and we all say things we don't mean on occasion. However, saying anything along these lines to the child with Asperger's Syndrome will have a long-lasting, damaging effect, possibly for the duration of his life. Why? Because, quite simply, he will believe every word of what you're saying as *the truth*. This will perpetuate in undue anxiety, stress, and upset that will persist over time. Your child may take personally criticisms you think mild or trivial. He may cry, pout, or sulk for hours or longer. If you are a parent short on patience and prone to such irrational outbursts, be prepared for your child to withdraw from you more and more until you are shut out completely. Spanking, slapping, hitting, or grabbing will produce results equally as damaging.

DID YOU KNOW?

The following ways of disciplining all kids also have application to your child with Asperger's Syndrome, but only after you are certain you've effectively communicated your expectations in ways he or she best understands: giving a time-out, temporarily withholding a privilege such as using the phone, computer, or TV; withholding allowance; and grounding.

Being sent to endure a set time limit in a private time-out area (or one's bedroom) or forfeiting certain privileges are acceptable, concrete forms of discipline used for all children with typically positive results.

The Right Time to Put Your Foot Down

Knowing when, how, and how much to discipline your child with Asperger's Syndrome can be quite challenging. You may be filled with worry for your child and her future. You may be learning more about becoming her strongest advocate. In so doing, you will need to find balance in your role as a parent and disciplinarian. There may be a fine line between being an effective parent and being perceived as zealous or coddling of your child.

Your child's diagnosis is a label that describes a sliver of who that individual is as a human being. Your child is many other things; her diagnosis does not exclusively define her (remember the self-fulfilling prophecy). In valuing your child's gifts and talents concurrent with understanding her diagnosis, be cautious about going to extremes. You have every reason to be a strong advocate on behalf of your child and in protection of her rights. But this does not exempt her from being disciplined by you or, where appropriate, by child care or day care providers, or educators.

Overprotectiveness

Some parents can become overprotective. They may make frequent excuses for their child's words or actions. And they may not discipline where most others agree it to be warranted. When this occurs—regardless of the child's way of being—the balance of authority shifts. The child gains more and more control while being protected in a sheltered environment with little to no discipline.

A BETTER PARENTING PRACTICE

Remember that kids are kids. You would never do anything to intentionally endanger your child; but, as much as you might wish to keep all your children safe from any harm or wrongdoing, sometimes life's most valuable (and enduring) lessons come courtesy of that famous institution of learning and life experience known as the school of hard knocks.

The Latin root of the word "discipline" means "to teach." Parents who are overprotective and do nothing to discipline their child are teaching some very artificial life lessons that will significantly hinder their child in the real world. One mother openly despaired that she envisions caring for her son with Asperger's Syndrome for the rest of her life. This may indeed be the case if she micromanages every aspect of his life.

The Dignity of Risk

There is what is known as the "dignity of risk." It speaks to the luxury we must allow persons with different ways of being to make long- and short-term mistakes, but not without support and guidance. This will be a great challenge to you as a parent who is naturally protective of your child. But it is the only way your child will be able to learn and prepare for greater independence in the future. Disciplining your child should be a teaching and learning opportunity about making choices and decisions. When your child makes mistakes, assure him that he is still loved and valued. In other words, focus on the issue at hand, not the person (i.e., yelling, "How could you be so stupid?" is not an option). Where possible, look for small opportunities to deliberately allow your child to mess up and make mistakes for which you can set aside discipline-teaching time. It will be a learning process for you and your child.

How to Deal with Meltdowns

In addition to being certain that you are communicating your limitations and expectations in as direct, clear, and concrete a way as possible, you will have to take into consideration three other areas before you discipline.

The inability to communicate—to articulately express oneself—in ways that are effective, reliable, and universally understandable is the first meltdown trigger. The other two meltdown triggers fall under the umbrella of communications as well.

The second meltdown trigger is pain and discomfort. That is, severe physical pain and discomfort that is not being communicated in ways that are effective, reliable, and universally understandable.

The third meltdown trigger is mental health issues. That is, significant mental health experiences that are not being communicated in ways that are effective, reliable, and universally understandable.

Communication Is Everything

The latter two areas fall under the communication umbrella because communication is *everything*. If you cannot express your physical or mental pain in the moment, then that obstacle is a communication issue. One or any combination of these three areas, communication, pain, or mental health, is what drives the junk behaviors—not Asperger's Syndrome. That's the good news. If you've succumbed to believing stereotypes about Asperger's, then this revelation may come as a surprise to you. Simply because your child has Asperger's, it does not follow that he will automatically manifest some or all of the junk behaviors as a direct result of Asperger's. This is an untruth; otherwise, such behaviors would be listed as Asperger's criteria in the *DSM*. Because your child is inherently gentle and exquisitely sensitive, she may be particularly prone to being vulnerable; she may be more susceptible than neurotypical individuals to experiencing issues of communication, pain, and mental health.

Dealing with the Meltdown Areas

But these vulnerabilities are not directly affiliated with the diagnosis of Asperger's Syndrome. They are by-products of the Asperger's experience in some—not all—children. The three meltdown trigger areas—communication, pain and discomfort, and mental health issues—are of such great importance that each topic will be explored in detail in this book. In order to be an effective parent and disciplinarian of a child with Asperger's Syndrome, you will need to comprehend each of these areas fully and place them in the proper context of any given situation. This knowledge will aid you in laying a foundation for prevention in order to minimize your intervention.

A BETTER PARENTING PRACTICE

All the resources of your parenting wisdom and expertise may be drawn upon in making respectful speculations about what might be driving a meltdown. Your child may find it extremely difficult or impossible to clearly articulate all the factors and nuances that came to bear upon her loss of control. Don't push her; try to be supportive and figure it out together.

All of parenting is a judgment call. At every moment, you are put in the position of making your very best respectful guess. In striving to be a good parent, you hope that your thinking will be right more often than not. Inevitably, you will make mistakes, and you may hear about them in no uncertain terms direct from your child. Can you be open to good listening? Can you find it in yourself to recognize that—even as the adult in the relationship—your child was right and you were wrong? If you are able to apologize in those moments in ways that are genuine and sincere, you will be rewarded with a bond.

Perhaps the best philosophy to share with your child when it comes to your role as a parent and disciplinarian is this: You may not always get what you want, but, sometimes, you can get what you need.

Chapter 6

Communication Is Key!

10 Things You Will Learn in this Chapter

- Exercises that will help you relate to your child.

- About receptive language and your child's challenge to understand what others are communicating.

- How to adapt your communication tactics so your child can process information better.

- How you thinking exclusively in imagery can help you understand your child.

- To slow down and carefully measure the amount of information you give your child at one time.

- Simple questions to ask yourself when you want to know if you are communicating effectively.

- How your child absorbs information differently.

- That eye contact is not important when it comes to comprehension and why.

- How to build trust and deal with disappointment.

- Why subtleties of language are especially challenging for your child and how to help him/her sort through slang, sarcasm, innuendo, and irony.

How Would You Feel?

In the last chapter, we discussed the three meltdown triggers that typically drive "behaviors" in children with Asperger's and autism. You will recall that the most significant of those three areas was the inability to communicate in ways that are effective, reliable, and universally understandable. When any one of us is feeling overwhelmed by circumstances that are unpredictable and that spiral out of our control, we may find it very difficult to verbally express ourselves in this situation. For example, think how you would feel if—all in the same morning:

- You oversleep because the alarm didn't go off.
- You have no hot water for a shower.
- You realize you're out of coffee.
- You don't notice that your pants have an obvious fabric snag until you're in the car.
- The entrance to your freeway exit is detoured due to construction.
- You can't find a parking space once at work.

When you finally get inside your workplace, you are likely feeling one or all of the following:

- Angry
- Upset
- Disoriented
- Short-tempered
- Depressed
- Anxious
- Stressed

Upon your arrival at work, what do you instinctively want to do? Find a friend or confidante as soon as possible in order to vent, and tell them about your morning. But where would you start? If you are feeling emotionally stressed or overwhelmed, you may be feeling like a huge, confused mass of all the feelings listed. You may not have the words to describe your frustration, or you may be completely inarticulate in the moment.

How Would You React?

If you can't get it all out in a way that is effective, reliable, and universally understandable, your frustration will continue to build. Now suppose someone unaware of your experience approaches you and makes a demand that is time-sensitive ("I need this within a half-hour!"). Everything you're feeling will escalate until you release it some way. You may do this by:

- Yelling or screaming
- Swearing
- Throwing something
- Breaking something
- Pulling something off the wall
- Clearing off your desk with a sweep of your arm
- Sitting and crying
- Avoiding the situation by disappearing to the bathroom, lounge, or smoking area
- Going numb and not responding to anything

Fortunately, such overwhelming experiences are rarities for most of us. But isn't it curious how many of these reactive behaviors are similar to the list of Asperger's Syndrome "junk behaviors" outlined in the last chapter? If anyone accused you of being unprofessional or even violent in manifesting such behaviors, wouldn't you defend yourself by explaining they were communications of your tremendous angst, that you were coping the best way you knew how? Fortunately, this scenario played out over the course of a few hours one morning. But you may use it as an analogy to understand how most kids with Asperger's feel in trying to cope and get through each day when it comes to navigating communication.

DID YOU KNOW?

Sometimes you may find that parenting a child with Asperger's who is overwhelmed means simply abandoning all expectations of trying to understand what just happened in favor of providing a gentle hug or allowing your child to have a good cry or personal space to temporarily shut down. You may find that these unspoken communications that you provide will have as much, if not more, impact than your verbal communications in the moment.

Your child may be quite challenged in her ability to process receptive language, that is, understanding what others are communicating. You may be frustrated by her apparent unawareness of the social repercussions of interrupting or saying something with brutal directness. Conversely, her idea of communication to others, or expressive language, may be skewed from what is considered the norm. Let's examine both perspectives.

Adapt Your Tactics

It is important to understand how your child with Asperger's Syndrome thinks and processes information. According to a number of self-advocates with Asperger's, we may speculate that many individuals with Asperger's are visual thinkers. This means, quite literally, they think in constant streams of images and movies—not Hollywood movies, but life-event "memory" movies. This way of thinking is very different from most others. You may think in pictures too, perhaps more so if someone specifically directs you to do so by saying, "Picture this," or "Imagine this." It may be an unnatural way of thinking for you without putting forth great effort, but it is a flowing, seamless, and natural manner of thought for many people with Asperger's or even autism.

A BETTER PARENTING PRACTICE

As a fun little role-reversal exercise, set aside time for a game with your child. Request that he describe the rules to his favorite video or computer game (or some other element related to his passions). Ask that he read up to four paragraphs, plowing right through without pause, while you listen silently. Once he is finished, you draw exactly what he has described, and see how close you get in accuracy. It may be eye-opening for you!

Thinking in Imagery

If you were to think exclusively in imagery, and you were in conversation with someone, then you'd likely require some process time to mentally "call up" pictures and movies based upon your life experiences in order to follow what the person is saying. If you are discussing something relatively familiar or even appealing, then the flow of pictures may be effortless. But what if your communication partner is relating new information for which you have no prior knowledge or experience? You would have to be especially attentive and try to listen very carefully to make sure you understood clearly. Concurrently, you would be attempting to call up or form mental images to equate what you think the person is telling you (which is perfectly obvious to them).

Give Your Child Some Time

Now, given a similar situation, what if you are a child with Asperger's and your communication partner is your parent or other adult in authority? If the adult doesn't "get" the way you think, you will be set up for failure when given multipart, verbal instruction. As a society, we have been conditioned to communicate with lightening-fast speed and to expect the same in return. But the child with Asperger's will need process time to catalog the sequence of steps being communicated and make a facsimile image or movie; give your child this time.

It Can Take Time

If you're communicating something new and different to the child, then assimilating the information and translating it into images and movies will take time. Your challenge as a parent is to slow down and carefully measure the amount of information dispensed to avoid confusion. If your child is unable to visualize what you verbally communicate, he is less likely to retain it.

What It's Like

You've experienced something similar when you've been lost and stopped to ask for directions. You may have quickly learned that you asked for more than you bargained for if the person who gave you directions slowly built, layered, and embellished the information until you could not keep track of the list of verbal information. Apply this scenario to the child with Asperger's Syndrome and you can understand how easy it would be to blame her inability to correctly follow through on noncompliance, or "bad," behavior.

Because your child may be a pleaser or have a flat affect, you may be unable to tell through body language or facial expressions if she understands—even if she says she does. If you wish to be certain *you've* communicated in ways that are effective, reliable, and universally understandable, take a few moments and go through these steps:

- Rethink what you intend to communicate. Can it be simplified?
- Before giving your child instruction, ask her to prepare to make pictures or movies of what you're conveying. Check back on this during your communication by saying something like,

"Can you see it?" or "Do you see what that's
supposed to look like?"

- Slow the pace of your instruction—especially if
  it's about something new and different.
- Allow for process time in between steps of
  instruction. Given how we've been conditioned
  to interact with others, this will be tough to do,
  but necessary.
- Ask your child if she's ready for more.
- After you've finished talking, give your child a
  chance to ask clarifying questions.
- Ensure your child's understanding of what
  you've communicated by asking her to describe
  what you've just said.

Like the driving directions scenario, be cautious
about overloading your child with too much information all in one shot. As your child's parent, you will be
able to best gauge how much or how little your child
can absorb at once.

Eye Contact Is Very Important

Be advised that many children with Asperger's will not
be as successful as they could be when given instruction
if they are required to make direct eye contact concurrent with your delivery of instruction. Many parents
command direct eye contact of their neurotypical children by saying something to the effect of, "Look at me
when I'm talking to you." Society has ingrained in us
the belief that if you make direct eye contact in conversation, you are listening carefully and paying close

attention. The twist is that for the child with Asperger's Syndrome, the opposite may very well be true.

Absorbing Information

The child with Asperger's who is across the room from you and appears not to be listening may be taking in nearly all—if not everything—you are saying, as opposed to the child who is compelled to make direct eye contact to "prove" he is paying attention. Why would this be so? Remember that your child is likely extremely visual in how he assimilates and absorbs information. When you speak, your face is in constant motion and there are many, many visual detractors, such as your eyes and glasses, your hair, your jewelry, your mouth, saliva, tongue, and teeth, and your clothing, not to mention other contributing factors like your breath and cologne.

Your child will be tremendously challenged to pay attention and listen if he is distracted by one, some, or all of these visual details. Your child will be faced with complying with the social expectation of making direct eye contact everyday outside his own home. Reflect carefully upon your ability to be flexible where direct eye contact is concerned, especially when giving directions. Your child may surprise you. If you feel that direct eye contact is non-negotiable in your family, then find compromise in:

- Seeking opportunities to make direct eye contact attractive or appealing, such as holding some favored item up near your face, while requesting eye contact

- Accepting your child's need to make fleeting eye contact, look away, then look back
- Accepting your child's "ballpark" approximation of direct eye contact if he stares at your ears, mouth, or some area of your face other than your eyes while you are talking
- Accepting your child's need to look away from your eyes in order to formulate a thoughtful, intelligent, and articulate response to you

Building Trust

Your child may be very dependable. That is, she does what she says she's going to do when she says she's going to do it. Because your child likely interprets others' communications in a very literal sense, she will expect you to do the same. In communicating with your child, it will be important that you do what you say you're going to do by keeping your promises—you'll be held to it! If you consistently overlook, cover up, or excuse your broken promises, you are chipping away at any trust your child has placed in you, and your relationship will grow ever distant.

DID YOU KNOW?

How often have you said to your child, "When I say no, I mean no"? The child with Asperger's says what he means and means what he says with the same definitiveness. That is, no means no and yes means yes. Your child's anxiety and frustration will likely escalate if you repeatedly ask the same question or ask him to change his mind without explanation.

If you must break a promise, apologize to your child as soon as possible and let her know precisely when you will fix the situation or make it right. If you approach such interactions in this respectful manner—and follow through as you said you would—your chances of being forgiven are far greater than if you do nothing.

Making Sense of Social Interactions

Now that we've talked about the way your child will best receive information, let's explore how she may best express communication. As you've just learned, your child may be very literal in her way of being and in everything she does and says. Part of her challenge in making sense of social interactions is to assume some flexibility and understanding when others are not as rigid.

Casual Promises That Confuse

People commonly make promises they have absolutely no intention of keeping. People say things all the time that *sound* friendly and sincere—and they may be genuine in the moment—but they get distracted, forget, or get involved in other things and never follow through. Some of these popular idioms include such "catch phrases" as, "I'll call you in a few days," "Let's do lunch real soon," or "I'll stop by to see you in a couple of weeks." They haven't intentionally mislead you, and most people shrug them off when these social dates don't come to fruition if they haven't already interpreted them as weightless, social conventions. They are in the same vein as asking, by rote, "How are you?" without really expecting to hear a rundown of how someone *actually* is.

Meanwhile, the person with Asperger's is waiting for the other party to come through and make good on the promise. With each day that passes with no communication, the person becomes more hurt, confused, or upset. Some folks probably forget making such comments as soon as they say them, or would be a bit surprised to be called on the carpet about them. You will need to counsel your child in this peculiar nuance of neurotypical behavior, especially as he enters his teen years—a time when people rely less on their parents and interact with greater social freedom.

Subtleties of Language

Another great challenge your child may grapple with is in understanding the flow of typical, everyday conversations. The language most people are accustomed to using may get "lost" on the child with Asperger's Syndrome. This is because everyday interactions are peppered with subtleties including:

- Slang (Example: "He lost his head!")
- Sarcasm (Example: "You're so smart!")
- Innuendo (Example: "They slept together last weekend.")
- Double-entendre (Example: "She's all that and a bag of chips!")
- Irony (Example: "Be sharp or you'll be flat.")

Most people learn to understand these subtleties by osmosis—simply by experiencing a reasonably typical upbringing in which they've automatically inferred meaning into previously unfamiliar idioms. They use body language and other cues to interpret the real meaning of the words. Many children with Asperger's are not privy to this "social code" and require your gentle coaching to decipher it.

A BETTER PARENTING PRACTICE

As a child, do you remember making up words to bridge your confusion when you didn't understand all of what others were saying during the National Anthem, the Pledge of Allegiance, or the Lord's Prayer? In hindsight, how many of the phrases you thought people were reciting were nowhere close to the actual language? Now reflect upon how it might feel to think the way you did then when trying to assimilate everyday conversation.

We all occasionally need such clarifications because we are all more alike than different. For instance, if someone said to you, "Duck," would you know how to interpret it? Would you look around for a bird, or would you physically lower your head to avoid being hit by something? Based on your past experience, the chances of being struck might seem higher than your chances of seeing the bird, and therefore you might "duck" your head. But it was a split-second judgment call.

Real-Life Scenarios
Here are two different, real-life scenarios involving boys with Asperger's that illustrate how slang is fre-

quently misinterpreted. In the first situation, a mother kept her distance in observing her young son's interaction with a baker when placing the order for his birthday cake. The boy responded well to questions such as, "What flavor icing would you like?" and "What flavor cake would you like?" But when the baker asked, "And what would you like your cake to *say*?" the very surprised boy exclaimed, "Are you crazy? Cakes don't talk!" In a worst-case scenario, one boy became a target for some older boys at summer camp. One of them told him to go jump in a lake—so he did, fully clothed. The boy jumped into the lake because:

- The other boy was older and perceived as intimidating or in authority, so the boy did as he was told (being a "pleaser").
- There was a lake there so it didn't occur to the boy that his tormentor could be referring to anything other than that lake.
- He was unaware of the slang expression that means the same as "Buzz off" or "Get lost."

Make It a Game

These expressions will need to be taught to the child with Asperger's. As an exercise, you may wish to sit with your child and develop a list of words and phrases that draw inspiration from the previous list of subtleties in language. It will be helpful if you are prepared to give examples for each item on the list. Your child will be greatly amused if you are able to share your own experiences of misunderstanding someone's meaning and intent, and ask your child to provide his thoughts about what you might've done differently, or how you would know better next time. When discussed as a "game" in this manner—and outside of real-life, potentially threatening, or scary situations—your child will likely feel comfortable and at ease deconstructing social idioms. Reinforce that it is always considered acceptable to politely request that someone repeat what they've said, or ask for clarification by simply stating, "I don't know what you mean. Can you please say it another way?" By doing this, you can help your child become adept at cracking the social code.

Strategies for Social Progress

It is easy for your child to misunderstand communications and do something other than you intended, or react with frustration when she tries and fails. Your child may be additionally challenged when interacting with peers and others because she:

- Has difficulty understanding the rhythmic flow of conversation.
- Talks off topic or interjects information that doesn't fit the moment.
- Is direct and honest and, in so being, is offensive to others.
- Doesn't understand how to maintain personal space.
- Has trouble deciphering people's body language.

There are a number of concrete strategies you may explore to address such issues.

Debriefing

Try debriefing social situations that were confusing or upsetting by privately, gently, and respectfully deconstructing them portion by portion. Request your child to model his recall of others' body language and facial expressions, or model them yourself and ask, "Is this what you saw?" Once you identify the breakdown in communication, you can better explain what transpired. You may wish to take the subtle language that was originally confusing and exaggerate it in an obvious way. Once your child "sees" it, talk about the less exaggerated communication originally used.

Learning with "Comic Strip Conversations"

Carol Gray, a special educator, has developed "Comic Strip Conversations," a wonderful, visual cartooning technique whereby you and your child literally draw—comic-strip style, panel by panel—social conversations using voice balloons to contain dialogue. Gray encourages using a color-coding system to identify emotions for further clarification. Many kids with Asperger's enjoy drawing, and this strategy is a safe and comfortable way to give your child control in deconstructing social misunderstandings or ideas to apply in the future. It is also a *visual* way to show turn taking in conversation, approximate comfort-zone distance from others, and how people's conversations can become jumbled and overlap when someone interrupts too frequently or disrupts the flow by talking off topic.

Making Lists or Videos

Develop a written list of key phrases that your child can use as a socially acceptable entry into conversation. There can be a hierarchy in the sequence of phrases such that they may flow into broader, larger conversations, such as "Hey, what's up?" "How's it going?" "What's new with you?" "What did you do over the weekend?" "What did you watch on TV last night?" Such standard questions also promote turn taking that includes eye contact (where possible). If your child gets stuck, she may also fall back on using typical "scripted" but kid-acceptable responses such as "Cool" or "That's awesome."

A BETTER PARENTING PRACTICE

To support your child using video to deconstruct his social interactions, do it as naturally as possible. If your child knows you are singling him out, he may "overact" and play to the camera unnaturally. Try videoing at family gatherings or picnics, at parties, while playing games, or during other activities. Always watch the video with your child in privacy.

You may also wish to consider videotaping. The caution here is that none of us see and hear ourselves as others do, and it can be quite disturbing for any one of us to watch ourselves on video. If you wish to try it, ensure that you have your child's permission. It may also be helpful not to single out your child but to naturally capture him engaged in some activities with others. Be certain that any debriefing you do with your child occurs in a gentle, unconditionally accepting environment. This was the case for one teenage boy videotaped during a discussion group at school. When he privately viewed the video of himself, he was astounded that he came across very differently than his personal perception of himself, and after that he worked to tame and refine his presentation style.

Writing

Many people are better at expressing themselves in writing than through verbal communication. Here is where computers are a tremendous benefit to kids with Asperger's. The computer is liberating because your child is free from social pressures with regard to immediacy of response, body language, facial expressions, personal space issues, and eye contact in conversation. Using e-mail to communicate with others *is* social! With e-mail, you can respond in your own time. You may be amazed at the incredible and eloquent global and personal insights your child types out in her own time and in the safety and comfort of her own home.

Many kids with Asperger's feel so socially inept that in-person "talk therapy" or group counseling is oftentimes ineffective. Try reaching your child with pressing questions and concerns by sending her an e-mail; you will get a reply that may surprise and enlighten your own understanding of the situation at hand.

Chapter 7

Teaching Your Child about Health

10 Things You Will Learn in this Chapter

- About different feelings of pain your child might experience and how he/she might deal with them.
- How to understand how much pain your child is in.
- How many children with Asperger's endure debilitating pain that goes undetected, unreported, and untreated.
- The two most prevalent forms of pain for children with Aspergers.
- What to do if your child has severe allergies.
- How gastrointestinal issues can plague your child and how you can help.
- About potty training and toilet issues specific to children with Asperger's.
- To teach your child that reporting pain is very important and how to do it.
- How asking the right questions might bring about shocking answers.
- How emotional and mood disorders affect children with Asperger's differently.

Feeling Pain

Of the three meltdown triggers discussed earlier that drive behaviors, experiencing pain and discomfort is extremely significant. This is because pain affects behavior—in us all. Think of the last time you were sick and feeling significant pain or discomfort. Was the pain a symptom of flu, migraine, menstrual cramps, a pulled muscle, or some other physiological condition? Now, think of how being in such pain manifested in your behavior. Perhaps you:

- Were especially hypersensitive to light or sound.
- Just wanted to crawl under the covers and stay there.
- Lashed out or snapped at loved ones.
- Lashed out or snapped when anyone made a demand of you.
- Just wanted to be left alone.
- Felt especially vulnerable.

Once your brain recognized the signals your body was sending it, you sought relief from the pain because you wanted to feel better. You also knew that relief was available to you. In assuming personal responsibility for your health and well-being, you took medication, pampered yourself, slept, or made a doctor's appointment. You did these things with the expectation that the pain would be alleviated in short order and you would return to feeling "normal" once again.

DID YOU KNOW?

At times, some individuals have difficulty verbally communicating their pain or the exact point of its origin. Others may not know how much pain they should endure before telling someone. The opportunity to access visual alternatives to speech such as pictures, written language, and scales of pain levels and intensity may be especially useful in addressing this issue, especially in young children.

Now Consider This

But what if the pain was not treated and allowed to persist? Suppose relief was not immediate or an option? Revisit the previous list and consider how your behavior might intensify the longer you had to endure pain. Not only would you feel lousy, you would also feel disoriented and distracted. Your attention focused on trying your best to cope and manage the pain that threatens to overwhelm you at any moment. In short, slowly but surely, your mental health would be impacted, eroded, and, over time, seriously impaired. Your ability to function, care for yourself, or interact with others with a measure of quality would be greatly reduced. Your self-esteem would suffer as well and you might not care about your appearance. The culmination of feeling physical pain would converge with mental anguish, leaving you weak and vulnerable.

Now, reflect on your child's experiences with pain. Take your own experiences and multiply them using this perspective and you may quickly understand how debilitating the experience of enduring pain may be for your child, especially if the pain goes undetected, unreported, and untreated.

Issues that Plague Children with Asperger's

Allergies and the consequences of untreated allergies are one of the two most prevalent causes of pain for children with Asperger's. The challenge is that many parents do not recognize this and see their child's symptoms in isolation, if at all. For example, the child with Asperger's may frequently experience ear blockages and ear infections (not unlike other children), sometimes from a very young age. Perhaps the child manifested outwardly visual symptoms such as red, sore, or draining ears. The child may have been treated with antibiotics or had tubes put in her ears to relieve pressure. More often than not, the ear problems were one symptom within a cluster of other symptoms, indicative of untreated allergies.

In addition to ear blockages and infections, the child with Asperger's may also manifest symptoms of allergy such as:

- Headaches and migraines
- Red, itchy, or runny eyes
- Sinus pressure over or under eyes
- Congestion and runny nose
- Swollen glands
- Sore throat
- Coughing and sneezing

Upon careful investigation, you may discover that several of these symptoms manifest together at the same times of the year. The culprit allergens could be absolutely anything—from one indicator, such as seasonal pollen, to an entire and exhaustive collection of many unknown indicators. While you may have been treating one or two symptoms, you may not have been addressing the bigger picture, that is, the chronic allergies.

DOES THIS SOUND LIKE YOUR CHILD?

Err on the side of caution. Take a moment to reflect upon the last few meltdowns your child endured. It might be that she was experiencing physical pain and discomfort that triggered her behavior or otherwise contributed to her in-the-moment communication of extreme distress. Take note of any physical symptoms apparent at the time.

Treatments

Treatment is available to prevent and relieve many of the physical side effects of severe allergies, like those listed, but testing is sometimes necessary to determine the allergen type and degree of severity. This may be problematic for many children with Asperger's, especially if they have had unpleasant experiences with doctors who were not as patient or sensitive as they should have been. Some of the testing and treatment may involve drawing blood or doing allergy skin testing, which may sometimes be an overwhelming experience and, ultimately, perhaps not worth the potential trauma.

Pediatricians do often treat children with suspected allergies without allergy testing though. And they then reserve allergy testing for those children who don't respond to standard allergy medications. When allergy testing is necessary, allergy skin testing is not usually painful when performed by a pediatric allergy specialist.

Lastly, you can try to allergy proof your home, concentrating on common allergy triggers and anything you think makes your child's allergies worse, which might include dust mites, mold, pet dander, etc.

Gastrointestinal Issues

Another prevalent factor that drives pain and discomfort in children with Asperger's and autism is gastrointestinal issues. That is, severe gas and cramping, bloating, constipation, impaction, and diarrhea. A number of such children have an inability to properly digest dairy and wheat-based food products (among others), such that the enzymes from these foods "leak" through the gut and into the bloodstream, potentially creating an adverse reaction described by some as an "opiate" effect. In clinical trials, the dairy products are referred to as "casein," and the wheat-based foods are referred to as "gluten."

Parents may find themselves frustrated with a child who seems "inappropriately" or embarrassingly gassy or who seems to have bowel complaints. Again, the child is not being deliberately difficult; there is a legitimate issue that is driving pain and discomfort.

Could an Infection Be the Problem?

As with pursuing the treatment of allergies, there are options that range from restrictive to less intrusive forms of treatment. In some instances, a bacteria or parasite of the lower gastrointestinal tract may be responsible for creating these issues, especially if your child also has chronic diarrhea. This can be an excruciatingly painful experience that may cause a child to double over in pain. If the child is unaware of the root of the problem or doesn't know how to describe the pain in the moment, his "behavior" may be misinterpreted instead of correctly identified as a communication. Consult with your pediatrician or family doctor to determine the appropriate treatment to eradicate all traces of these infections.

Treating Problems

The procedures to determine the cause of the gastrointestinal tract maladies may be very physically intrusive. You may wish to explore less invasive methods of intervention as an alternative first if the child has not had a good history with medical practitioners. These may include:

- Pursuing a diet free of dairy and wheat, in partnership with the child and in consultation with a dietician or nutritionist.
- Obtaining stool cultures to test for bacteria and parasites.
- Avoiding foods with dyes or preservatives.

- Cutting back on red meat proteins in favor of chicken, fish, or other food options.
- Considering soy and other substitute foods, perhaps for a select time frame, to note any cause and effect.
- Using any over-the-counter products designed to aid gas relief or alleviate bowel distress, like fiber-based additives.
- Increasing fluid intake, especially water, may prove helpful as well.
- Increasing consumption of natural food fiber found in fruits and vegetables.
- Promoting massage and exercise.

Fears Surrounding Toileting

Some gastrointestinal concerns may be compounded by the child's fears and anxieties around toileting. Children with Asperger's Syndrome tend to be careful observers. Most will attempt toileting—especially urinating—in their own way and in their own time, just at a time later than what might be considered developmentally appropriate. Still others may appear to deliberately wet or soil themselves. Please be patient. Recall the positive philosophies and know your child is not deliberately being insubordinate; he really is struggling and feeling just as frustrated as you. Here are some thoughts that may help clarify your understanding of toileting issues in the child with Asperger's Syndrome:

- Your child may be frightened by the toilet, believing that he may fall in and get sucked down.

- Your child may be overwhelmed by the loud roar of a flushing toilet.
- If the child is not feeling safe and comfortable and in control, withholding body waste is one way of independently attempting to gain control.
- Your child may panic, believing that in making a bowel movement, she is shedding a vital, living piece of her body.
- Your child may be in a "perfectionism" mode, unwilling to admit his need to use the toilet when asked, or embarrassed to confess the need.
- Your child may not be well-connected enough with her body to consistently receive the physical "signals" or pressure indicating the need to evacuate waste.

To counteract these and other issues, it will be important to deconstruct the whole toileting process for your child using very basic, *visual* information. The *Once Upon a Toilet* books have the right idea in explaining the process of how and why the body rids itself of waste to very young children, but these books may be far too immature for your child. You'll need to adapt this concept, expanding upon it by using your own visuals such as graphics explaining the human digestive system, naming internal parts of the body.

Be Supportive and Helpful
Reinforce with your child that the process of eliminating waste from one's body is natural. In partnership

with your child, explain that *everyone* with whom your child interacts does this regularly and that it is natural—family, doctors, caregivers, teachers, and others all do this daily. You may be surprised to find this is a significant revelation for your child, especially the child who is struggling to match the perceived perfection of the adults in her life. Just as important, also ensure you reinforce that using the toilet is a *private* matter. It is not to be discussed freely in public; it should only be discussed with close, trusted individuals (list them in writing), usually if there is cause for concern like constipation, impaction, diarrhea, etc.

Some children will also want specific assurances about exactly what happens to their waste once it gets flushed away—where does it go and what becomes of it? You may need to research this yourself, or look it up on the Internet with your child. If you are uncertain if your child experiences the sensations indicating the need to evacuate waste, first ask her about it. Talk about the ways in which you know your body gives you the appropriate signals, and plan daily, gentle exercises designed to better connect your child with her body, such as yoga, breathing, and stretching exercises.

Additionally, there may be adaptations and accommodations you can make in giving your child control in toileting, such as adjusting the water pressure to avoid a rushing roar when the toilet is flushed or partnering with your child to select a new toilet seat that is more comfortable and makes the toilet opening less foreboding. Implementing some or all of these strategies should enable your child to attain greater comfort in his approach to toileting.

Reporting Pain—An Essential Step

As we've discussed, it is absolutely critical that the child with Asperger's grows into an adult able to identify and advocate for her own relief from pain. As with toileting, it will be useful to visually explain how the brain and body usually work together to send signals indicating pain. Sometimes the signals are accompanied by visuals that help reinforce that something is wrong, such as a bleeding cut or blister. Other times, the signals may be exclusively inside the body and unseen, just felt. The Internet or your local library should be a resource in accessing images, books, or videos that describe this physiological process.

Reasons for Not Reporting Pain

Still, there are some children with Asperger's who are inconsistent in reporting pain, if at all. Here are some speculations as to why this may be:

- Your child may not understand that there exists an unwritten social expectation that we all report pain and discomfort in order to gain relief.
- Your child may not realize that what he's feeling in the moment is anything any different from what anyone else feels.
- As with toileting, your child may not have a nervous system she feels fully connected with,

such that the pain is delayed or not "registering" properly.

- Being inherently gentle and exquisitely sensitive, your child may have been severely traumatized by experiences with doctors and nurses so that she considers enduring the pain the better option.

One mom shared the following observations about her young son:

People had told me that Alex had a high tolerance for pain. He broke his arm one day, and the teacher saw it happen, but he just winced and went on. Later, she realized he couldn't use the hand. I started realizing that Alex had experienced pain from an early age. He knocked his four front teeth loose at three years, and then hit them again at four and five. (We now know he has no depth perception and was extremely far-sighted.) He probably had experienced pain as a part of daily life without being able to explain it. I went home and asked Alex about his body. He felt sure he wasn't registering pain well, but when he came down to it, he reported what turned out to be plantar warts, which are sometimes quite painful.

Another young boy suffered with mild asthma for several years of his young life. Upon gaining diagnosis and treatment, his first exclamation was to say, "Mom, I didn't know it wasn't supposed to hurt when you breathe."

Ascertaining pain in your child may prove especially challenging if she is often expressionless. During an assessment with a teenager with Asperger's, she stunned most everyone in the room. When asked about pain and discomfort, she rattled off a long laundry list of ailments with which she coexists on a daily basis. No one would have ever guessed her struggles simply by looking at her demeanor; her facial expressions revealed nothing. It was a matter of asking the question in order to receive the answer.

A BETTER PARENTING PRACTICE

On occasion, medical professionals are not patient, gentle, or sensitive to our needs. Until your child can advocate for her own needs, never hesitate to advocate on her behalf. If necessary, cancel an appointment, switch doctors, call in, or write a letter of (tactful) complaint, or otherwise diplomatically make your child's needs known.

One young man in his twenties was grappling with severe, debilitating dental pain. He adamantly refused to seek treatment because of prior traumatic experiences with the dentist. (Who among us *doesn't* feel anxiety about dental appointments?) Not seeking medical treatment for his pain became the path of least resistance for him. However, his pain was chronic. He opted to self-medicate by using nicotine, marijuana, and alcohol.

Teaching Your Child Self-Advocacy

In addition to educating your child about how the body works when communicating pain, it will also be important to partner with your child in gaining self-awareness and control leading to lifelong self-advocacy. This means reinforcing that it is good and desirable to identify and report one's own pain. The message to the young girl who endured a litany of daily pains (and others like her) needs to be loud and clear. It is *not* okay to live with chronic pain. Other thirteen-year-old girls don't live with it, it is not normal or typical, and relief is available once proper diagnosis is made. Imagine how detrimental enduring chronic pain would be for this young girl if she were thirty-three instead of thirteen. How productive would her life be, and how would others characterize her "behaviors"?

Additionally, it will aid tremendously in quelling your child's anxiety if you endeavor to demystify the entire concept of going to the doctor *in advance* of an appointment. You may do this by partnering with your child to consider doing the following:

- With your child, schedule a time to drive to the doctor's office before the appointment day.
- Assign your child the responsibility of reading you driving directions to and from the office location, noting street names and landmarks.
- Once at the office, empower your child by allowing him to take photographs inside and out. Review these later at home (where your child feels most comfortable), eliciting details from him.

- If at all possible, arrange to meet the doctor, the nurse practitioner, and—at the least—the receptionist. Again, provide the opportunity for your child to take pictures.
- Suggest that your child photograph a typical private room, being remindful that, next visit, you may not get that exact room but one very much like it.
- Before making the trip, partner with your child to develop a list of questions to ask the doctor, nurse, or receptionist. If there's the opportunity to do this, allow your child to take the lead in gleaning the information desired.
- Arrange to get as many specifics about the appointment as possible, including approximate wait time and details of any procedures, along with literature and other visuals.
- Discuss flexibility of time frames with your child, and empower him to keep track of the time during the actual appointment.
- Gain clear information about the tentative sequence of events in order to visually list these out with your child (he can bring this list with him on appointment day).
- Because of downtime while waiting, suggest your child bring something to read or work on, possibly to share with the doctor as well.
- Schedule a pleasurable activity for your child to follow the appointment. Ensure that the activity occurs regardless of how well you think your child does or if he "earned" it.

DOES THIS SOUND LIKE YOUR CHILD?

Doctors' offices can be very busy settings with appointments often backed up and running late. Time permitting, call before leaving to confirm your scheduled time. Don't be surprised, though, if, upon finally meeting with the doctor, your child doesn't give him or her a good dressing down for "being late"!

If this sounds like a lot of prep work and a significant investment of time, it is. But in the long run, this initial investment of time upfront will go a long way in supporting your child to feel safe and comfortable and in control. Empowering him to take the lead during this process promotes his ownership and sense of self-advocacy.

Your Child's Mental Health

You will recall that mental health is one of the driving factors in "behaviors." It is also the most ambiguous factor. Psychiatry, the practice of ascribing probable mental health diagnoses, is not an exact science. Determining a mental health diagnosis is predicated upon educated attempts to pin down the intangible. There is no single psychiatrist who can unequivocally state the precise mental health experience of any given individual; the experience is unique to each individual, so it may manifest in many nuances. The best a doctor can do is make an educated best guess based upon her professional expertise. She does this in conjunction with observing and interviewing a client and consulting the Diagnostic and Statistical Manual (or other clinical documents) to narrow it down to a diagnosis based upon a series of symptoms—what the client reports of his experiences and how he presents during the interview.

There is a long-standing stereotype that perpetuates the belief that "junk behaviors" in people with different ways of being (including Asperger's Syndrome) are merely by-products of those experiences. But knowledge is power and, as a parent, your approach should be one of prevention instead of intervention. Remember the self-fulfilling prophecy? Understanding how to successfully avert its vicious cycle will directly impact your child's mental health.

Make It Obvious

To begin with, it is important to outwardly express your love and caring for your child in ways that she understands, using concrete pictures, words, and actions paired with validating statements. For example, you could set aside times to spend with your child and sing her favorite songs or create an arts and crafts project that builds upon one of your child's most passionate interests, while acknowledging that you love her and love sharing this kind of time with her. Together you are creating life movies for future replay.

Unconditional Love

Reinforce to your child that your love is unconditional—a tough concept for many kids, let alone the child with Asperger's, to grasp. Explain that, even though your child may make mistakes or do things you disapprove of, your love is constant and will never waver. Be certain to praise your child's accomplishments, gifts, and talents often. Highlight his successes, and tell him how very happy and proud he makes you feel. Tell others about the amazing things he's accomplished as well, and, with his prior okay, make such comments publicly in his presence. Ask him to show you exactly how he did what he did and tell him how much you've enjoyed listening to him (even if it gets long-winded and tedious). Tell your child with Asperger's Syndrome that he or she is beautiful—not just physically beautiful, but truly beautiful inside. Tell him that his inner beauty is that of being a good human being who wants to give of his gifts and talents to others. Discuss how this inner beauty is the most valuable of all, far more important than physical attractiveness

Why all the emphasis on glorifying your child? In doing so, you are incrementally fortifying the child with Asperger's Syndrome by laying a foundation of strong self-esteem. This will serve as ammunition as your child grows and enters adolescence and beyond. Never underestimate the power and long-lasting effect of your most loving words and actions. Your child will retain and replay the most memorable of such experiences for the rest of her life. They will buoy her when she needs it most.

How to Get Help

It is often difficult for parents to see the forest for the trees. That is, people tend to recall major, cataclysmic behavioral "events," as opposed to being objective—stepping back to notice a trend or cycle of symptoms.

Some parents may also struggle with issues of guilt or denial. This is where consulting with a professional will be of great value.

DOES THIS SOUND LIKE YOUR CHILD?

There's a phrase used to describe untreated mental health issues: "The longer the needle plays on the record, the deeper the groove becomes." Some parents become oblivious to the obvious because of their guilt or denial. If you believe that your child demonstrates highly unusual or out of control behaviors, please actively seek timely clinical support.

Finding a Psychiatrist

The challenge may be finding a clinician who is abreast of recent "best practice" trends (what is presently acknowledged as the "right," or respectful, approach) and does not buy into stereotypes that your child's behavior results from being a kid with Asperger's. As with seeking the initial diagnosis for Asperger's, you may encounter difficulty in locating a psychiatrist who meets this criterion. This is where networking with other parents or Asperger's/autism organizations in your area may be helpful. As before, be prepared to travel, especially if you live in a rural area and resources are sparse.

Preparing for the First Visit

If you believe your child is experiencing a mental health issue, prepare yourself and your child for the appointment with the psychiatrist just as you would for the appointment to interview for a diagnosis (review these steps in Chapter 3). In addition, it will be of greatest benefit to a psychiatrist if you come prepared to discuss *symptoms* and not *behaviors*. This text has provided you with the language used to describe symptoms—euphoric mood, grandiosity, and the like. This is language a good doctor will recognize and understand.

What to Tell the Doctor

You know your child best; a psychiatrist is especially vulnerable to whatever you do and say. After all, unless you have a previously established rapport, she's meeting you and your child for the first time. You have an obligation to your child to be direct and concise and to stay focused on discussing symptoms. When you enter a doctor's office venting with lots of storytelling about how difficult it was last weekend when your child trashed the house, punched his sister, and threw a TV out a second-story window, you are discussing behaviors. It may be natural to want to do this, especially with someone whom you hope will understand, validate your experience, and provide you with answers.

Be Careful with Your Words

However, in describing behaviors, you've just significantly broadened the doctor's challenge; the previously listed "behaviors" can crosswalk to dozens of potential diagnoses. When this occurs, you risk your doctor "falling back" on ascribing stereotyped diagnoses like schizophrenia, borderline personality disorder, obsessive-compulsive disorder, oppositional defiant disorder, or intermittent explosive disorder.

These and others are commonplace in people with differences. Yet, we are all more alike than different, and mental illness is an equal opportunity offender. It is not selective, nor does it distinguish between brains. Doesn't it make sense that mood disorders, the most prevalent mental health experience for us all, would also be typical of folks with different ways of being?

You can prepare for an initial appointment with a psychiatrist by doing the following:

- Organize your child's symptoms as best you can by breaking them into categories for depression or bipolar to start.
- After listing out the previous two, list symptoms of anxiety and PTSD.
- Keep everything brief and concise—to one page if possible. Use numbered or bulleted entries so your doctor can easily scan the information.
- Be prepared to discuss your family's mental health history (including alcohol and substance abuse) and any cycles you have noted in your child.
- Let the doctor know if your child has already been diagnosed with a condition, such as ADHD, and you disagree with the diagnosis, especially if he didn't respond well to standard treatments. Some children with Asperger's are first thought to have ADHD and actually have worsening behavior problems when they are put

on stimulant medications, such as Adderall or Ritalin.

- Become educated about medications traditionally used to treat mood disorders, like Lithium, Depakote, and Tegretol, and other newer mood stabilizers such as Lamictal, Zyprexa, Trileptal, Neurontin, and Topamax.

- Get information about some of the newer atypical antipsychotic medications, such as Risperdal, Abilify, Zyprexa, Seroquel, and Geodon, which can help to treat mood swings and aggressive behaviors.

- Ensure that you have a way that your child will either participate in a gentle, respectful discussion with the doctor, or ensure that there is someone with whom your child can stay in a waiting area while you discuss specifics that may be very upsetting for your child to hear.

Consider Short-Term Hospitalization

If your child's symptoms manifest in extreme, violent behavior that causes him to seriously endanger himself or others, you may also need to carefully weigh the option of a short-term commitment to a psychiatric hospital in order to keep him and your family safe. The goal of a short-term hospitalization is to stabilize the child as soon and as safely as possible prior to discharge back to his family. There, he may receive observation and treatment in a controlled environment. The treatment may include medication to stabilize him and help him to feel level again.

▶ DID YOU KNOW?

It may be a distinct and profound relief for your child to realize that what has been compelling him to "be bad" isn't his fault. Remember the circular wheel of the self-fulfilling prophecy? Self-loathing, guilt, and remorse can become its lubricant. Wherever possible, partner with your child to educate him while gently encouraging him to exert control over his mental illness to the best of his ability.

In gaining control over violent behavior, antipsychotic medications will likely be prescribed. Such medications are usually strong sedatives, intended to "slow down" the child so that he will be manageable and less of a threat to himself and others. Such antipsychotic medications may include Thorazine (chlorpromazine), Mellaril (thioridazine), Serentil (mesoridazine), Prolixin (fluphenazine), Stelazine (trifluoperazine), Haldol (haloperidal), and Loxitane (loxapine) among others.

Fortunately, many of these medications have been replaced with newer "second-generation" atypical antipsychotics that have fewer side effects, such as Risperdal, Abilify, Zyprexa, Seroquel, and Geodon. They are still powerful medications though and can have significant side effects though, including drowsiness and weight gain. For children with violent mood swings, the benefits may outweigh the risks of taking one of these medications though. Risperdal is now approved by the FDA to treat irritability associated with autism in children between the ages of five and sixteen years of age.

Your role as a strong advocate for your child is to be educated about the names of medications, the reason for their prescription, their duration and desired effects, and any adverse side effects. This is not a time to be shy, self-conscious, or feel inferior—don't be afraid to ask and re-ask important questions or to request a second opinion if you are feeling dissatisfied. If at any time you suspect your child is experiencing mental health issues, it is imperative that you take aggressive, proactive action to address them before the situation escalates into a severe crisis.

Prevention Not Intervention

Many people with Asperger's—adults and children— grapple with anxiety, depression, and other mental health issues. Psychiatric diagnosis and medication may become a way of life, especially if the individual receives clinical benefit from this approach. The caveat lies in parents believing that this is the sole answer. Remember, the key is prevention, not intervention. It's never too early to shower your child with adoration and accolades that will become a foundation of strength for him. Finding a medication regime that is a good match is a trial and error process that may take time, sometimes months or years. However, medication isn't everything; if your life is still lousy and there is no positive change, medication can only do so much.

A BETTER PARENTING PRACTICE

Creating an informal circle of support around your child (that also includes her) will provide her with an unconditional place of communion with those who know and care for her best. The circle should create a positive, personalized plan of support—a map or blueprint—to complement the IEP (Individual Education Plan), psychiatric treatment plan, or other types of written documents designed to assist your child. Assign roles, responsibilities, time frames for implementation, and gather regularly over food and drink.

Teach Self Advocacy

If you have confirmed that your child is suffering from a mental health problem, empower her to become self-aware in order to grow into a strong self-advocate. Her ability to recognize her own symptoms and know her individual needs is of great importance. What follows are examples to foster mental health self-advocacy in your child. Here is a sample story that your child may read and personalize by illustrating it.

There are over 100 different chemicals in your body. Each chemical must have balance with the others so you can feel your best. Sometimes, the chemicals are unbalanced. When there is too much or too little of one chemical, it can change the way you think, feel, and behave. When this happens, you may be unable to control your thoughts, feelings, or behavior until the chemicals become balanced again. Your body may need medication to help the chemicals become balanced again.

Imbalanced Emotions and Mood Disorders

Everyone has many different feelings. Some feelings may make you very happy. Other feelings may make you sad enough to cry. Feelings like happy and sad can also be called moods. Most people have moods that go from very happy to very sad. But when the chemicals in your body become unbalanced, your mood can become more high or more low than usual. When these changes happen it is called a mood disorder, because the moods are out of the usual order.

The mood disorder has two parts with different names. The highest mood is called mania. The lowest mood is called depression. Because mania and depression are two parts of one mood disorder, it is named bipolar disorder. Bi means two. Polar means poles, like the North Pole or the South Pole of planet Earth. Bipolar means two different poles that are opposite from one another. We think of being happy and sad as opposite from one another.

How Does It Feel?

People who have mania say it feels like their body is racing hard inside. They can be happier than usual. Or they can get so upset that they break things. Or they may hurt themselves or others even if they don't really mean to. They want to keep doing things they like to do without stopping. It may be hard to sleep or eat or think clearly. They may even believe they have superpowers and can do impossible things. This is harmful.

People who have depression feel sadder than usual. They may cry easily. They stop doing things they used to like a lot. They may feel tired all the time, no matter how much they sleep. Some people who have depression may not feel hungry. Others may feel hungry a lot. They may feel so bad inside that their bodies really hurt, and they can't find a way to make it better. It is like having an engine inside you that just won't start no matter what.

Bipolar disorder happens in cycles. This means that at certain times a person can feel either mania or depression. After the mood goes away, they may feel okay again. If someone has bipolar disorder, it is very important that others understand how it feels. It is especially important that a doctor understands how it feels.

Another strategy that has been effective is to partner with the child to draw the mental health problem as he envisions it. What has worked with many children is to imagine a car in which you are competing for control of the driver's seat. In the driver's seat, you're in control of the car, but if your mental health problem takes control, you may be bumped to the passenger seat, with limited control—or worse yet, you're bumped to the backseat or the trunk. One young teen drew his bipolar as a skeleton dressed in leather; because he was into NASCAR, he actually enjoyed drawing the car in great detail. Many such children are able to accurately tell, on any given day, exactly *where* they are positioned in the car. The ability to independently articulate one's own mental health experience will be of lifelong value for your child.

Chapter 8

Is the School Ready for Your Child?

10 Things You Will Learn in this Chapter

- What school is really like for your child.

- About special educational services available to your child and family.

- About the Individuals with Disabilities Education Act.

- How to formally request an evaluation of your child by the school and what the testing entails.

- About the stigma of special education and what the term means today.

- To set up a team meeting with the school and develop an Individualized Education Plan, or IEP.

- The services you and your child are entitled to after having been deemed eligible for IEP services.

- How to develop goals for your child based on his/her needs and strengths.

- Reasons why a school district might resist an IEP for your child and how to challenge this.

- About alternative educational systems and how you might want to consider thinking outside the box.

Diagnosing Children and Special Needs in School

One distinct advantage to obtaining a formal Asperger's Syndrome diagnosis for your child is that she will be eligible to receive certain educational services and supports. (As Asperger's is not an "officially" eligible diagnosis, according to federal law, your child's eligibility may be determined with a diagnosis of autism, other health impairment, or speech and language impairment. Keep reading to find out more about this.) One reason why school districts are sometimes unable to provide such services is because the child has not been identified as needing support services. In some instances, even if educators are aware of your child's diagnosis, some may misinterpret your child's individual attributes. Sometimes, children with Asperger's are accused of being "lazy," inattentive, or simply not applying themselves to the best of their abilities. This may be true in some children (as it may be for any neurotypical child) but such accusations have become so overused that they are Asperger's stereotypes. In other examples, schools may overlook the child who maintains during the day (by being quiet or compliant) but has legitimate educational needs.

Other children, who are fine academic achievers but experience meltdowns during the day, may be "missed" by school districts for needing a select educational program. Instead, such students may be placed in classrooms for children with emotional disturbances.

Individuals with Disabilities Education Act

A safeguard to ensure that your child's educational needs are met by your school district is the Individuals with Disabilities Education Act, known as IDEA. (In this instance, the word "disabilities" is a necessary evil, and it shouldn't define how you or the world view your son or daughter.) IDEA is the federal law that guarantees your child's entitlement to a Free and Appropriate Public Education (FAPE). The types of disabilities covered by IDEA include the following:

- Autism
- Mental retardation
- Hearing impairment (including deafness)
- Speech or language impairment
- Visual impairment (including blindness)
- Serious emotional disturbance
- Orthopedic impairment
- Traumatic brain injury
- Other health impairment
- Specific learning disability
- ADHD

DID YOU KNOW?

Your child's most pressing needs, as you see them, may not be academic at all but social. This subtlety may be challenging for your child's educators to concede, and this may lead to unfair labeling of your child's way of being. Remain confident of the fact that you know your child best, and advocate on her behalf.

As noted, some school districts may oppose the need for an Individualized Education Plan as it applies to the child with Asperger's based upon this list, or based upon the failure to recognize the educational implications of Asperger's. The last bullet, "specific learning disability," may apply to your situation if your child "does not achieve commensurate with his or her age and ability levels," or if your child "has a severe discrepancy between achievement and intellectual ability" in one or more of the following areas:

- Oral expression
- Listening comprehension
- Written comprehension
- Basic reading skills
- Reading comprehension
- Mathematics calculation
- Mathematics reasoning

These are all areas identified by IDEA (specifically in 34 CFR, section 300.341). As you can see, many children with Asperger's may readily qualify for educational support—especially the comprehension portions—based upon the breakdown definition of "specific learning disability." Other school districts may use the designation of "other health impairment" to qualify a child with Asperger's. This is where a comprehensive evaluation by a psychologist, psychiatrist, or other qualified professional experienced in diagnosing Asperger's Syndrome will be most helpful.

Getting the Evaluation

The school district should offer to provide such an evaluation if you do not already have a diagnosis for your child. If not, the process can be initiated at your request. Ensure that you make this request in writing, include language giving your consent to an evaluation, and retain a copy for your records.

The conclusions of the professional conducting the evaluation will likely show discrepancies between your child's intellectual abilities and his ability to achieve in any of the previously listed areas. This is vital in order for your school district to appropriately qualify your child for an educational program designed to meet her needs. (Districts are mandated to have "Child Find" policies in effect to identify, locate, and evaluate children who may be protected under IDEA.) In this way, you can begin to establish a proactive, working partnership with your school district.

A comprehensive evaluation by a professional experienced in identifying Asperger's Syndrome should also contain recommendations for how you and your child's educational team might move forward in developing a plan to support your child.

Special Needs, Special Education

The phrase "special education" can be very frightening to some parents. It may conjure images of your own recollections of classes tucked away in far corners or the basement of a school, and peopled exclusively by children with mental retardation. Remember FAPE? Part of the acronym stands for "Appropriate Education." Placing your child with Asperger's Syndrome in a stereotypical special education classroom with children not on par with his educational intellect (meaning those with mental retardation) would be inappropriate. (In fact, IDEA provides that, wherever possible, all children with disabilities, including mental retardation, should receive their education alongside typical peers such that there is gradual momentum toward phasing out special education classrooms.)

DOES THIS SOUND LIKE YOUR CHILD?

Many children with Asperger's Syndrome communicate their desire to just fit in and be like the other kids. And yet, some may have daily needs for which they are unready, unable, or unwilling to articulate. Be prepared to creatively discuss options and opportunities to include your child throughout the school day.

So if someone from your school district happens to slip and use the phrase "special education" in reference to your child, don't freak out immediately; this person has most likely used the term *generically*. But do ask for specific clarification. Nowadays, special education can take many forms of service, and may be as subtle as supporting your child's learning comprehension using a teacher's aide, for example.

Developing a Plan

The evaluation for your child should determine his special education (or related service) needs and will generate an appointment for a team meeting to develop an Individualized Education Plan, or IEP. The IEP is the document that will detail, in writing, an individualized approach to meeting the unique needs of your child. The team should include:

- You and your spouse.
- One regular education teacher.
- One special education teacher.
- A school representative who can make decisions about the delivery of services (usually the building principal).
- Someone who can interpret the evaluation results as they apply to your child's educational instruction.
- Other participants with special expertise or knowledge of your child.

Your child may also participate if he chooses to be present. Participants with special expertise may include a parent advocate knowledgeable about IDEA and the IEP process, a professional consultant who specializes in developing IEPs, or a professional consultant who specializes in Asperger's Syndrome. Finding a specialist can be a crucial issue, and it can be frustrating to both parents and school officials when one is not accessible.

Your Child's Specific Needs

At this point in our collective learning curve (and depending upon your geographic location), it may not be realistic to have the expectation that your child will be taught by a teacher experienced in educating students with Asperger's Syndrome. Because you know your child best, you may become fiercely protective and defensive of what you believe your child needs. On the other hand, most willing and cooperative school districts may lack such expertise and may be of the position that they are doing all they can. Such disputes are addressed later in this chapter.

The Evaluation Process

If you have requested that your school district evaluate your child in writing, the district must comply, and this process should be completed within sixty days after your first written request. If they don't, they must give you information on your due process rights so that you can appeal the decision and figure out how to get your child evaluated. Your pediatrician and/or child psychiatrist may be able to help you with this process.

Following this, the district will ask that you sign a "Permission to Evaluate" form. The evaluation should be completed within sixty days after your *original written request* (that contains consent from you to evaluate your child) *not* sixty days after you've signed the permission form. Once the evaluation is completed, a team meeting should be convened to review the evaluation. You should receive your child's evaluation well in advance of the team meeting, but no later than ten days prior to such a meeting. This team meeting may also serve as the first IEP meeting if you wish.

If your child has been deemed eligible for services, IEP team members should be identified, and the first meeting should occur within thirty calendar days of the original determination of eligibility. The completed IEP must then be implemented within ten school days. It must also be reviewed yearly and can be revisited in a team meeting *upon your request* outside of the annual meeting date. The IEP must also be in effect for your child at the beginning of each new school year.

A BETTER PARENTING PRACTICE

Don't be intimated to request an advance, blank copy of the tool that will be used to evaluate your child. It will help you understand the special education services process and provide indicators of areas in which your child may excel or fail. One excellent Web site with information on special education law is *www.wrightslaw.org*.

Creating an Individualized Plan

The initial IEP meeting is the time and place to develop the document that will be the blueprint for your child's educators. The draft document should be transcribed into the final document immediately following the meeting. It should include:

- A cover sheet with a sign-in page listing all participants.
- An acknowledgment of your child's eligibility.
- An area for you to sign, acknowledging that the school district has provided you with a copy of your rights during the process, known as "procedural safeguards."

- Basic information such as your contact numbers and address, your child's date of birth, and anticipated year of graduation.
- A list of "special considerations," such as visual or hearing impairment, behaviors that impede your child's ability to learn (or that of classmates), and communication issues.
- A summary of your child's strengths (his passions and interests).
- A summary of your child's needs (those areas in which he requires special support).

A strong IEP team should be able to find a balance between your child's strengths and needs. Too often, such meetings can focus upon issues that others may perceive as "behavioral" or emotional disturbances. When this occurs, teams get sidetracked and lose their focus. Teams may digress and deteriorate. Parents may leave feeling angry or upset, and the self-fulfilling prophecy is perpetuated. For this reason, and particularly in very sensitive situations, it is advisable to have a professional in attendance who fits the bill of "other participants with special expertise or knowledge of your child." In partnership with the team, this person can help keep things focused on your child as a child first and foremost.

Establishing Goals

The next step is to set IEP goals that are specific to your child's strengths and needs in order to track your child's educational progress and ensure that the team is implementing what they committed to doing. The goals should be realistically achievable for your child and written in such a way that they are easy to track or "measure," in order to see your child's growth and keep the team accountable. For example, an appropriate goal for a kid with Asperger's of any age might be in the area of developing computer skills (if she's not already a computer wizard). While this may sound rather generic, the spin here is to make it specific to your child's Asperger's. The purpose of the goal should be clearly stated, such as a goal for accessing the Internet: "The student will develop skills to use a computer to communicate, to gain information, and to increase social relationships independently three out of five times." Next, objectives to meet the goal should be identified in sequence. The sequence for the computer goal might look like this:

- The student will learn the functions of the computer, including turning the computer on, signing on to the Internet, and using the keyboard and other functions while exploring her passions (such as searching for information about insects as they relate to a lesson plan).
- The student will create and access a file and store information she wishes to save in the file.
- The student will learn methods to access social interaction through electronic media (e-mail).

A method and schedule of evaluation for each goal objective should also be included. For example, the method for the last objective listed might read, "During computer learning opportunities, the student will be afforded opportunity to increase social interactions by learning to use e-mail and other communication avenues."

A BETTER PARENTING PRACTICE

Consistency in communication of your child's needs from school year to school year is imperative. Don't take for granted that strategies, adaptations, and accommodations discussed but not recorded in your child's IEP will be carried over unless they are clearly documented. This assures accountability as well as consistent support.

A goal for enhancing self-advocacy might address your child's ability to identify and communicate her sensory sensitivities in the school environment. A goal or objective might read, "The student will be able to communicate in a socially acceptable manner the specific change she requires in her educational environment four out of five times." The method should include supporting the child to identify environmental stimuli that are irritants and detract from learning.

Modifications of Programs

The IEP should also list "program modifications and specially designed instruction" that may include elements incorporated into goal areas, which team members should bear in mind. Such a useful list may include examples like:

- Limit or eliminate visual and auditory stimulation and distractions in the learning setting.
- Explain directions clearly, in steps and with visual representations.
- Allow extended wait time and processing time.
- Use photo depictions where possible instead of cartoons or drawings.
- Provide advance notice of schedule and special situations.
- Be consistent with the expectations established for the student.
- Provide an individual, weekly schedule to follow.

The IEP document will also indicate the projected date for implementation of services, the anticipated duration of services, and any revision dates. Specifications addressing how the school district intends to report IEP goal progress should be clearly stated. There must also be a statement reflecting why your child's current educational placement represents an inclusive environment as fully as possible (LRE, "least restrictive environment") as opposed to an alternative placement.

Challenging the System

Some parents and school districts are possessed of more experience and greater expertise in educating children with Asperger's than others. There will always be kinks to iron out in the IEP process, and these can usually be addressed at the annual IEP meeting or at a requested reopening of the IEP. When parents encounter resistance from a school district it is usually because the district:

- Doesn't "see" the Asperger's Syndrome as a viable diagnosis
- Believes your child's challenges to be exclusively behavioral issues
- Believes they are meeting the goals and objectives of the IEP to their best ability

Where parents resist a school's efforts, it is usually because they are extremely frustrated that the school district doesn't understand Asperger's and, as a result, doesn't "get" how to educate their child. Ignorance can be used as an initial excuse, but it is not an acceptable long-term excuse. School districts have a responsibility to make provisions for the continuing education of teachers and to seek outside technical assistance and expertise as necessary. Parents have a responsibility to serve as a resource concerning their child's strengths and needs, as well as directing the district to viable resources and expertise wherever possible. When the circumstances of educating your child through proper implementation of the IEP goals and objectives become less than satisfactory, you have recourse available to you, provided by the IDEA law.

Steps Toward Change

You may request an Impartial Due Process Hearing (in writing) at any point in which disagreement arises about the delivery of education to your child. This includes your child's identification, evaluation, placement, or implementation of the IEP.

The Impartial Due Process Hearing takes place with an "impartial hearing officer." The hearing officer is the "fact finder" who hears all the evidence and makes a ruling on the issues presented during the meeting. Such individuals are employed by your state government's education office of dispute resolution, and are of varied background and position, such as former education administrators, attorneys, or psychologists.

A BETTER PARENTING PRACTICE

If you are in conflict with your child's school district, you need not go it alone. Connecting with other parents who have "been there, done that" should be of enormous benefit in your endeavor. Some such parents, who have become quite savvy to special education law, may be available to support you in meetings as parent advocates. You can also hire a specialist, including a special education lawyer or a child psychologist to accompany you to these meetings.

A hearing is to be held within thirty days of the request. The school district must forward a parent's request to the office of dispute resolution within five days of its receipt by the district office. The hearing officer's decision must be issued within forty-five days of the request for the hearing.

Be Patient

Be advised that there are often delays in scheduling or a hearing officer may not be timely in making his or her final determination to settle a dispute. During the dispute, the child in question is to remain in his current educational placement (unless he is a danger to himself or others). The hearing officer's decision may be appealed and taken to an appeals panel within thirty days. The appeals panel must render a decision within thirty days after the review request.

Taking It to the Next Level

Hopefully, such measures will be entirely avoidable, but if a parent remains dissatisfied after exhausting local administrative avenues, action may be brought in any state court of competent jurisdiction, or in any district court of the United States, as provided for in IDEA. There is no statute of limitations for commencing such action in federal court, but it is advisable to file as soon as possible. There may be time frame limitations for filing a case in your state court.

Moving to file a case is stressful, frustrating, and draining for all parties involved. However, court rulings can set precedent for changes in law to the benefit of all. Anytime significant change has occurred in how children with differences are educated, it has been at the instigation of passionate parents simply wanting fair and equal opportunities for their children.

Alternative Education

Hopefully, you will be a persuasive advocate when interacting with your child's school district. You just may be the person to educate and enlighten the professionals in your district if they require a better understanding of

Asperger's Syndrome. In some extreme instances, families have moved to another school district or another state in order to have their child attend a certain school program. Unfortunately, in addition to the stress on the whole family that this type of upheaval can cause, it also allows school districts to remain uneducated about how best to support students with Asperger's Syndrome.

The Delta Program

Some progressive school districts have developed alternative education programs available to those students that want them. One such example is the Delta program in State College Area School District, Pennsylvania. Since its 1974 inception, the Delta program has become a national model for alternative, "nontraditional" educational programming for eligible children from grades seven through twelve. Delta is founded on the belief that students are motivated to do their best when they are responsible for their own learning. Classes are not arranged by grade level, but by learning level, from introductory to midlevel to high level.

Delta is a partnership between the student, parents, and staff through shared decision-making. Enrollment does not exceed 200 students at a time in order for teachers, administrators, and support staff to provide quality, personalized interactions with students. Students are required to complete all state-mandated requirements for education the same as their peers. The program differs in that each student has an advising team (like an IEP team), and an open campus structure allows for flexibility, experiential learning, and community service projects.

Each semester, students in tandem with their advising team members design personal educational schedules by choosing from courses offered in required subject areas. However, as a guide, each course has a difficulty level that ranges from introductory to midlevel to high. When planning student schedules, the set number of credits required in each subject area is taken into account along with the difficulty level. In advance of course enrollment, each Delta student is aware of the course content, learning objectives, and the manner in which their work will be evaluated—all of which serves to promote independence and personal responsibility in learning. As an added incentive, further program flexibility is offered by allowing students to take certain classes in the regular high school or middle school, attend nearby Penn State University, or participate in other opportunities available through local businesses or technical schools designed to suit student-centered needs.

The Susquehanna Waldorf School Model

Another Pennsylvania educational model is the Susquehanna Waldorf School, which serves children in grades one through eight. It is founded upon the holistic philosophy of teaching the whole child, mind and body. The school considers that each phase of childhood requires different perspectives. This translates into seven-year spans, starting at birth through age twenty-one.

Throughout, the emphasis is about sequentially teaching what is good, truthful, and beautiful. By these standards, teachers honor the work of all children. The individual interpretations of each child are valued in balance with the contributions of others. Children are shown with care how to be discriminating, thoughtful, and prudent.

DID YOU KNOW?

The Regio Emilia model of education (such as that found in Grand Rapids, Michigan, and elsewhere) allows schoolchildren to guide the curriculum. The inherent sense of wonder and curiosity children have about how things work in nature gives educators a "jumping off" point. The child with Asperger's may fit well with a similar program in which interests and curiosities are valued.

Charter Schools

Most states have an educational option called charter schools, in which the school district has received a "charter" from the state. The charter provides rules, such as where it is located and the maximum number of students permitted to attend. With a charter, the school district receives the funding and allocations based on the number of students. The state Department of Education grants the school district funding to pay for teacher salaries, equipment, and materials to meet the individual needs of each student in a charter school.

Charter schools are considered "public schooling," and must abide by all state regulations. The charter school may have an emphasis on the arts or science with a smaller teacher-student ratio.

Virtual Charter School

Another innovative program, called a virtual charter school, uses the charter school model with a couple of differences. The virtual charter school is like a "public school in a home environment," but it is not the same as home schooling.

Former U.S. secretary of education William Bennett and some others started a company called K12, headquartered in McLean, Virginia. K12 provides the curriculum and management services; the virtual charter school hires the teachers and support staff. The head of the school, the controller, and a few others are employees of K12.

To attend a virtual charter school, the student's parents unenroll him from the local school district and enroll him in the virtual charter school. The school district funding follows the student and encompasses books, materials for art and for science experiments, a computer, and other materials. The student also receives a regular education teacher, a special education teacher, and an IEP, just as in the local school district.

The teachers become the educational supports working in partnership with the parents (who have the lead) to educate the child and ensure he or she takes all the state-mandated standardized tests. The parent must log time daily on a Web site and track the student's progress, such as what lessons he or she has completed; lesson plans are also received via the Web site. Frequent field trips, all of an educational nature, are planned as a way for the children, teachers, and parents to connect with one another.

Home Schooling

Home schooling may be another option to consider, but be cautioned that the parents who undertake it tend to report that it's a lot of work and social opportunities for the child with Asperger's are curtailed. Parents wishing to home school their child select the educational curriculum and design the child's program. An affidavit must be filed with the state Department of Education attesting to the home schooling program, and parents must submit documentation at the end of each school year showing that the student has completed either a set number of hours or days of educational programming per year (it may vary from state to state). Another requirement is that a portfolio containing the child's work must reflect that the she has made the equivalent of one year's educational progress.

Also, private schools or educational institutions affiliated with religious denominations may offer a more individualized curriculum with one-on-one instruction, but the cost of enrolling your child may be prohibitive.

Benefits and Disadvantages

Alternate educational placements may benefit the child with Asperger's Syndrome through smaller teacher-child ratios, leading to more individualized attention and quality assurance in your child's learning comprehension. Smaller class size may afford instructors the luxury of time to focus attention on meeting the unique educational needs of each child. Educational curriculum in alternate settings may also have greater flexibility and provide for enhanced opportunities to reinforce educational curriculum in ways that may be tangible and concrete for the child with Asperger's, such as regular field trips to museums, businesses, landmarks, and other community attractions. There may also be opportunity for creative programming in which the child may have myriad choices from which to select when planning class projects, presentations, or reports. Greater individualized attention may also mean that your child's personal passions can be used to underscore his learning.

A BETTER PARENTING PRACTICE

Be aware that some alternate educational placements that offer your child individualized guidance and one-on-one attention may only extend up until a certain grade level. You may need to determine if the transition to and from such a setting will benefit your child.

A disadvantage to alternative educational programming and placement may be the cost. If a newly designed program is considered, planning, implementation, and start-up time are all factors that may be deterrents for some as well. Social opportunities may be more limited with smaller or one-student classes unless efforts are made to compensate for this. Your local school district or state Department of Education should be able to provide you with details about a range of education program options, as well as funding options and obligations.

Chapter 9

Is Your Child Ready for School?

10 Things You Will Learn in this Chapter

- How to determine your child's needs and clarify them to the teacher.

- How educators should determine your child's strengths and build upon them.

- Strategies for linking a child's passions to learning opportunities.

- How to help your child make a visual imprint, allowing him/her to hold onto information more easily.

- About sensory sensitivity and how to avoid over-stimulation.

- How to help your child "fit in."

- Tricks to help your child feel more comfortable in the school environment.

- How to relax your child when it comes to the stress of school, homework, and other stressors associated with "being a normal kid."

- How to deal with bullies.

- About athletics and other activities that will build your child's confidence and give him/her an outlet.

A Typical Day

School presents an environment in which children are expected to be attentive listeners and ready learners. In addition, the school day provides numerous opportunities for students to spend time getting to know one another. It will be important that you, your child, and your child's educators have a clear understanding of the most salient points of communicating with a child with Asperger's Syndrome. Specifically, how educators communicate information and the process time they allot for it can make or break your child's ability to assimilate educational curriculum on a day-to-day basis. If your child is very passive or is a "pleaser," he may readily get swallowed up in confusion and misunderstanding—all the while giving the impression that everything's fine, until it's too late.

A BETTER PARENTING PRACTICE

Understanding how your child thinks and learns in her own words is a powerful alternative for some professionals who may perceive certain parents as over-zealous or overprotective. Encourage your child to privately write or type some of her personal thoughts about coping (without fear of getting in trouble).

How Your Child Learns

It will be crucial to communicate with your child and his educators, preferably prior to the start of the school year, in order to clarify your child's needs. Do his teachers have a clear understanding of what his needs will be (perhaps as dictated by the Individualized Education Plan), and does your child know what to do and say if he gets "stuck"? If you know your child to be a strong visual thinker and learner, ensure that any verbally communicated curriculum is reinforced with visuals. Some children cannot process visual and auditory input simultaneously without distraction; they are "mono-channel," meaning they cannot absorb what they are seeing and hearing at the same time and can only attend to one or the other. As many children with Asperger's Syndrome are so visual, this means there is potential for them to be distracted by everything in the room, so that they absorb only bits and pieces of the instruction.

In one instance, a young boy's school team was frustrated because they thought they were supporting him fully by assigning him a classroom aide. However, the aide was verbally reiterating the classroom teacher's direction in such a way that their words overlapped one another. The boy was receiving almost exclusively verbal instruction, out of sync, and *in stereo*! Now, consider his predicament in desiring to pay attention to his teacher, but knowing he must also attend to his aide. Layer on top of that the constant motion of a typical elementary school classroom setting and it was a recipe for disaster.

Your Child's Strengths

Many children with Asperger's Syndrome generally possess a number of strengths upon which educators may build. These include:

- A strong knowledge base for individual topics of passionate interest.
- The desire to conform to rules and boundaries.
- Retaining information best when it is visual, sequential, and linear.
- Best understanding logical, concrete topics of discussion.
- A willingness to please and to keep trying.

Your child may well benefit from a classroom aide in order to support her comprehension. It will be best—and nonstigmatizing—if *all* the children in class understand that the aide is accessible to them if they have questions or need guidance to reinforce the teacher's instruction. In this way, the aide's role is discreet.

DID YOU KNOW?

There are some truly wonderful school administrators and educators who love teaching and enjoy kids. You'll recognize them immediately because they will remind you of your child's gifts and talents. When this occurs, remember to validate their observations and courtesy.

Passions Can Help a Child Learn

It will also be important that your child's educators embrace the concept of building upon your child's passions. It is unrealistic to expect a classroom teacher to center educational curriculum around one child's passions; however, wherever possible, it will help engage the child if the teacher can artfully introduce elements of the passion(s) in the instruction. Strategies for linking passions to learning opportunities is best applied by your child's classroom aide or directly by you if no aide is assigned or available. All children are eventually confronted with educational concepts that are vague and indiscernible for them. Your job and that of the teacher (and aide) is to "coach" your child on the sidelines before sending him out into the game. That is, deconstruct the concept with which he is struggling by using his passion both before and after he's expected to learn and retain it.

A Helpful Example

For example, you might suggest that the names given to parts of plants also relate to the hanging vines in a Mario Brothers' computer game. Instead of asking that your child recite the textbook plant parts, request that he link the same information to the Mario Brothers' plants. He will retain this information, and with a gentle reminder, he will "call up" the knowledge when it's required (such as at test time).

Some children take this to extremes and don't realize that they are sidetracking a teacher's instruction with lengthy explanations of their passions (which can fuel educators to stereotype the passions). Children who do this need clear, concise, and *written* rules provided to them about when and where it's okay to expound upon their interests.

Learning by Doing

Your child likely has a strong associative link when learning. That is, she learns on the spot, in the moment while "doing" whatever it is, and will forever retain and "link" that experience with the moment. Many children with Asperger's think and learn this way. It will be important, then, to understand your child's struggles if educators wish to place emphasis on "pull out" programs or classes in which your child works one-on-one with an adult with the expectation that she process, retain, and apply what was just learned to the classroom situation. The two rarely mesh with success because of the strong associative link.

⟶ A BETTER PARENTING PRACTICE

When in doubt about how your child may best think and learn, think back on your own experience with "associations." Recall how certain scents or songs are forever linked in your memory to people, places, and life events and may be inseparable from those recollections.

A Visual "Imprint"

Your child will be poised for greater success if she can learn by doing in the moment and through incorporation of as many visuals as possible to reinforce it. In so doing, a visual "imprint" is recorded in her memory that, with gentle prompting, she can call up and replay. You may then incrementally build upon such pleasing experiences by relating them to something new and different. For example, you might suggest to your child, "Remember when we made homemade peanut butter?" (Give her process time to replay the mind movie.) Then continue, "The way a factory processes sugar cane is similar because . . ." You may be surprised at the quality of detail with which your child is able to relay information. She may become excited about taking a pleasing, fun learning experience and applying it to something novel.

The Over-Stimulated Child

Schools are fraught with environmental stimuli that can conspire to wreak havoc on your child's sensory sensitivities. Many children with Asperger's already torture themselves with anxiety about wanting to follow the rules, live up to teacher expectations, and get through each day without incident. In addition, they must grapple with having their senses assaulted throughout the day. In some instances—if the child is not yet a self-advocate, or if he is unaware of his own sensitivities— he may be unable to pinpoint exactly what triggers him to lose control. This is extremely common.

Fitting In

So many kids with Asperger's Syndrome are keenly aware of the social, educational, and environmental expectation that they blend in and "fit in." To compensate, they "hold it together" all day long as best they can. Once they get home, they finally release, lose control, and melt down in the safety of the home environment— where they feel most comfortable to let down their guard. This creates a perplexing situation for teachers who report to parents that their child seems "fine during the day." It also creates a frustrating situation for parents who may internalize their own self-doubts about something they must be doing wrong. It is no one's fault; the child is merely reacting to the relief at dropping the façade he's borne for the past six hours or more.

DID YOU KNOW?

You may be pleasantly surprised to learn that many environmental adaptations and accommodations can be low in cost or cost nothing. In fact, you may wish to apply them, wherever possible, to your own home in addition to those of friends, neighbors, or relatives.

Here are a number of suggestions that you will wish to share with your child's teachers in order to minimize the potentially hurtful environmental stimuli in typical school settings:

- Hallways can become extremely noisy and "echoey." Wherever possible, keep classroom doors shut.
- The volume of the PA system in the room may be too loud. If it's possible to adjust the volume, this can help. Same for the change-of-class bell.
- Classroom walls can be overstimulating and "busy" with decoration. If visuals cannot be streamlined, at least keep them somewhat static so the child with Asperger's can become accustomed to them.

- Consider felt pads under the feet of all classroom chairs as buffers against the constant scraping noise they make.
- Carrels or partitions around learning stations and computer centers are great for creating visual blocks on either side of a student and can also cut down some noise.
- Classroom announcements or posters like "Ten Great Ways to Treat Others" are most effective if transcribed and distributed to all kids (this makes them easier to retain when outside the room).
- Numbering classroom rules as written reminders for the child with Asperger's is a good idea, but publicly displaying them on a desktop is stigmatizing. Tape them inside a child's notebook or binder and refer to them discreetly.
- Focus on natural lighting instead of florescent lights when possible, using fewer overhead lights or adding alternate lighting such as floor lamps.
- Give the child with Asperger's advance notice of fire drill times so that she may brace herself for the noise. If she cannot tolerate it, small foam earplugs may help, or wearing Walkman headphones may diffuse the noise.
- Ringing classroom phones can be startling. Switch to a flashing light instead of a ring to indicate a call.
- Ensure that all students have advance knowledge of schedule changes outside of the routine, such as early dismissal or assemblies.

Implementing these measures will significantly help the child with Asperger's to "hold it together" in a more environmentally friendly atmosphere.

Getting through Homework

When you are young and extremely sensitive, school is your life, teachers are omnipotent, and homework is everything. Many children with Asperger's Syndrome generate undue stress for themselves by agonizing over homework to the point that they cannot be calm and rest because they feel so overwhelmed. Some may wail, cry, or hyperventilate because they believe homework to be a life or death situation. Parents and teachers may affirm that they know the child is capable of the work; however, this is not about incapability. The child with Asperger's Syndrome can be overcome with stress and anxiety by a litany of tasks that seem insurmountable. Being simultaneously confronted with homework, impending tests, and assignment due dates may fuel such a tremendous sense of frustration and futility that the child may be totally unable to discern where to even begin.

Problems with Homework

If your child becomes upset and overwhelmed when confronted with multiple homework assignments, he will require your support to break down the tasks (organized *visually* on a timetable that becomes the child's property) so that the assignments are scheduled in manageable portions. Reinforce that the child need only focus on the work scheduled for the allotted time slot. Your child's teacher will be an invaluable resource in helping to "map out" such a timetable into realistically doable bits.

DID YOU KNOW?

Your child may be stigmatized by peers if they perceive her as the "teacher's pet," or if she is acknowledged as "different" and unable to complete homework assignments. It's important to be discreet in cases where a child's homework assignment is modified from the rest of the class's.

A child's confusion and misunderstanding of directions can lead teachers to inaccurately label that child for his "behaviors." Their observations may focus upon some children's inability to complete homework. The refusal to complete a homework assignment in full may stem from the child feeling personally offended by what is being asked of her. If your child has demonstrated that she can master a concept, she may become offended when asked to demonstrate that capability by essentially "regurgitating" the same concept in various ways (via the homework). A compromise may be to allow the child to do fewer homework problems.

If the homework is going to be publicly reviewed aloud in class, parents and teachers will need to be more creative in conveying *why* completing the entire assignment is necessary. Or teachers could arrange to stagger the order of the assigned homework problems, with both student and teacher being aware of which problems she is most likely to be called upon to report.

Perfectionism and Anxiety

Some children operate in a "perfection mode" because they are "pleasers." They may relate better to adults with more advanced skills or they torture themselves trying to duplicate computer-generated examples in textbooks, like perfect handwriting, for example. Trying to be as perfect as adults appear to be, only magnifies the self-imposed pressure to comply with exacting accuracy. Tension and anxiety can balloon out of control for the child who must erase his work over and over again because it doesn't "match" the textbook or teacher's example.

If your child does this, he needs you to express, in writing and pictures, an understanding that *everyone* messes up and does things wrong *every day*. It may come as a groundbreaking revelation for your child to learn that his parents, teachers, relatives, doctors, and others don't do everything exactly right all the time. This is not giving him permission not to strive to do his best; it's a discussion about flexibility within rules and permission for him to go easy on himself. Your child will likely be absolutely tickled to hear your own stories about the times you messed up in school and lived to tell about it!

With patient support and practice, these homework strategies should help your child relax and focus.

Dealing with Bullies

Like it or not, many kids with Asperger's are perceived as different by their peers despite their efforts to blend and assimilate. Coming across as different can make a child a target in the eyes of those who prey upon the weak and defenseless. Many children with Asperger's become terrified and anxiety-ridden at the prospect of being bullied, especially during the transition to middle school and high school. As freshmen, they are younger than the other students who may traditionally give all incoming students a hard time.

When the Bully Is a Student

Many school districts have taken a no-tolerance approach to bullying, especially with the significant increase in school violence nationally in recent years. They have also developed written rules and guidelines about what is unacceptable student behavior and the consequences for not complying with the rules. Your child should receive such a written policy either in advance of the start of school or within the first week of school. If you don't have it, contact the school to request it. Having it may help soothe and appease your child's worries.

DOES THIS SOUND LIKE YOUR CHILD?

Providing your child with your school's written policy on bullying is not enough. She needs to know exactly whom she may trust to approach and confide in (which is hopefully any adult in the school). She will, of course, likely single out one or two closest school adult allies whom she knows will take her complaint seriously.

Facilitating partnerships that may lead to friendships (allies) will be critical, starting at an early age. Some schools also have a buddy system, whereby younger students are mentored or assisted by older, supportive students during an orientation period. You may also need to partner with your child to devise a way to hold a frank discussion with her teachers about the need for protection during the school day. Appropriate ways to cope with verbal and physical abuse need to be taught and rehearsed. Give your child a numbered list of actions to discreetly maintain in the event of an incident. The actions may include the exact phrases to use when telling her abuser to stop it, and knowing to whom bullying should be reported. Some children may also require coaching to learn how to recognize some forms of bullying that may be very subtle. Consider this story:

> *Luke Jackson, a young man with Asperger's, has commented on bullying in his writings.*
> Being different may not be a problem for me, or other kids like me, but it sure seems to cause problems for "normal" (ha!) kids. The result . . . bullying! I think there is some amount of bullying going on at all times, in schools everywhere. Some have it worse than others, but all have it. I was definitely bullied, and "it" was very painful at times.
>
> Always remember that "different is cool!" A lot of teachers and adults think bullying is "part of growing up," but I have written books, talked at conferences, and opened my life up on television just to let everyone know that people with autism in any shape or form are just as entitled to be themselves as anyone else in the world.

When the Bully Is an Adult

In some unfortunate instances, the bully is not another student but an insensitive teacher. One teenage girl with Asperger's honestly did not understand her gym teacher's instructions. After telling her several times (still in ways she did not understand), the exasperated teacher pushed the girl and said, "What are you? A retard?" This is, of course, inexcusable behavior and must be dealt with by counseling the child immediately to prevent the onset of post-traumatic stress disorder. The issue also needs to be addressed with the school administration so that the child is removed from that teacher's class and the teacher's behavior is addressed.

You may also need to counsel your child about reporting extreme cases of bullying; ensure that he is clear about what is good-natured kidding and what is unacceptable to endure.

Athletics and Playing on a Team

You may already be well aware that your child is not as physically agile as he may wish to be. It is common for children with Asperger's and autism to experience motor control challenges. It may be very difficult for some to make those brain-body connections necessary to physically produce a movement already envisioned in the mind. This can be very frustrating for all, especially the child who wants to succeed. It can also lead to a child being humiliated and publicly singled out as "uncoordinated." Many school gym classes are shifting away from picking sides for games, which is a blessing for the children who are consistently picked last.

Physically Frustrated?

If your child has experienced public embarrassment due to her inability to physically achieve on par with her same-age peers, it may be tempting for her not to engage in any form of physical activity at all. Instead, she may disengage from any such opportunities in favor of spending more time in isolation. This type of sedentary pattern is not healthy for any child, and can lead to self-image issues, worries about body type, and weight concerns.

DID YOU KNOW?

Many typical social interactions among children and teens include physical activities such as sports, dancing, skating, horseback riding, and others. If your child disengages from his peers, he misses out on these and he may be at risk for a sedentary lifestyle that may lead to weight gain.

As a parent you may recognize the benefits that regular physical activity can offer your child, but may feel torn. Some parents go to extremes in attempting to mold their unathletic child into a model of conformity. This kind of pressure to achieve in order to "please" can only widen the distance between child and parent when the child cannot live up to unrealistic expectations. You may have already witnessed, or read about, little league or soccer parents who create such hostility and anxiety for their children that the sport is no longer fun but a fierce, adult-level competition that is unpleasant for all.

In partnership with your child, decide upon some physical recreation activities that may be pleasing for your child to try. The child with Asperger's Syndrome will enjoy greatest success with athletic activities that are *self-contained* and *noncompetitive*. Such activities do not necessarily need to occur without partners and in isolation. It simply means that there is no race-to-the-finish time frame within which one must excel to score points. There is no winner or loser, and no undue pressure to perform.

Activities That Work

To start, build upon the movements your child already does well, even if it's simply walking. Being in or near water is extremely important to the vast majority of kids with Asperger's. The buoyancy of the water, the overall pressure it offers, and its solitude is enormously attractive to many. Would your child's health and motor coordination benefit from learning how to swim?

Martial arts also hold a special appeal for many children with Asperger's. Martial arts have a structured regimen with levels of achievement that promote self-discipline. Learning the moves in martial arts involves lots of visual repetition and incremental learning—something your child may already thrive upon. It also promotes making slow, deliberate, and methodical brain-body connections in order to be conscious of how all parts of one's body move and relate to one another. Tai chi is also effective in accomplishing similar goals. Your child can also proceed at her own pace and experience success as she moves up each level.

DID YOU KNOW?

More than a few children with Asperger's who have struggled academically or socially have experienced great success and pride through participating in a martial arts program. Moving "up" the tiered level of colored belts is a tangible, visual way for them to measure their achievements.

Activities similar to the discipline and coordination offered by martial arts include yoga, gymnastics, ballet, and dance. Other self-contained, noncompetitive physical activities include:

- Walking or running
- Horseback riding
- Bike riding
- Weight training
- Shooting basketball
- Roller skating or in-line skating
- Jumping rope
- Playing hopscotch

Adding your child's favorite music to any of these activities will be a good motivator and make the process that much more attractive. You may wish to participate with your child in some or all the physical activities he selects. Other partners may include siblings, friends, and relatives (cousins, nieces, nephews). These opportunities become ideal times for social interaction and connectedness, free from the pressure to achieve and score points.

▰▰▰▰ A BETTER PARENTING PRACTICE

Encouraging your child to participate in team sports may require "prerequisites" prior to sign-up. Simultaneous with your child's participation in self-contained, noncompetitive physical activities, facilitate opportunities for reciprocal interactions early on, such as sharing and taking turns during computer or board games. This may be useful in aiding your child to better understand the way team sports "work."

Playing on a Team

There will be times in which your child participates in an athletic activity as a member of a team, either by choice or as dictated by the structure of a class, like gym class in school. Being the member of a team can require that your child juggle a lot of things at once. It can quickly get confusing, perhaps for some of the following reasons:

- Although the team sport has rules, the activity is unpredictable.
- In the chaos and excitement, your child may forget the rules.
- Noise from spectators or teammates can make staying focused difficult.
- Your child may forget exactly who her teammates are.
- Your child may get disoriented about the location to score points.

Ways to alleviate some of these issues are to ensure that your child's teammates are distinguished in some way (usually by different-colored jerseys). Take time to go to the playing area prior to a game to familiarize your child with the surroundings, such as where the team will play, where spectators will be seated, and the location of the area where the team scores points. Being able to practice a team sport skill at home with you or siblings or friends can only help her develop confidence in her capabilities. She may simultaneously improve her ability to absorb and assimilate all that the game entails in a comfortable, unconditional environment.

Learning to be a Good Sport

Remember the perfectionism mode in which some children find themselves? This can also apply to the concept of winning and losing. Some children (including those without Asperger's) become so intensely hell-bent on winning that losing becomes its own drama, and the defeat represents personal failure.

Your child may have perceived that winning a game is the only option, and that losing is a "bad" thing, or that losing means she did something wrong. Granted, some adult role models are not helpful to this end either. How many of us have watched professional athletes on TV curse, spit, throw things, or start fights? When your child loses, he may internalize a lot of self-deprecating thoughts and feelings. His emotions may reinforce stereotypes he or others may have about him. This is, of course, harmful to his mental health and can deteriorate the quality of his social connections.

Keep Communicating Visually

You will be wise to communicate early on a balance between playing a game (especially as a team member) and winning. As always, you will want to communicate this concept *visually* in pictures and words. Be sure to include information similar to that discussed in the last chapter about perfectionism. Team members rely upon one another to cooperate and work together. No one wins all the time; it is impossible because we are all human beings. Two key lessons that your child may wish to remember are:

- You win some, you lose some.
- It doesn't matter whether you win or lose, it's how you play the game.

Not only can these phrases be used as responses to any catcalls of defeat from others, they may be used as effective analogies to "losing" or missing opportunities in any number of real-life circumstances.

In dialoguing with your child, be sure to distinguish a bad sport as someone who becomes angry at losing, someone who may yell and swear, cry loudly, or throw equipment. A good sport is still allowed to feel disappointed, but she knows there will be other chances to try again. A good sport is someone who can congratulate the opposing team with sincerity. Some things to say might be, "You played a good game" or "I'm going to try harder next time." A good sport tries his best during every game, whether he wins or loses.

▰▰▰▰ A BETTER PARENTING PRACTICE

Remember that, as a parent, you still have the right to apply fair, appropriate discipline after you believe you've communicated your expectations as effectively as possible and they are clearly understood by your child with Asperger's. If, for example, you've discussed, through pictures and words, the concept of behaving like a good sport and your child engages in an irretrievable meltdown after a loss, then it may be the time to consider your parental options.

As before, revealing one's Asperger's Syndrome and potential needs for accommodation to a coach or teammates is a personal decision of disclosure. Decide with your child if disclosing a diagnosis is helpful or stigmatizing. Perhaps simply being clear and specific when communicating an area of special need is all that is required.

Structure at Summer Camp

For many kids with Asperger's Syndrome, time that is unstructured can be problematic. It can lead to overindulgence in solitary passions, or it can lead to boredom from lack of intellectual stimulation. In a child's life, the greatest block of unstructured time is, of course, summer vacation. If your child is geographically isolated from other children or schoolmates during the summer, or community activities are not options (for whatever reason), you may wish to consider summer camp.

For the child with Asperger's who is inherently gentle and exquisitely sensitive, the notion of summer camp can be paralyzing. In her mind, it may involve packing up and leaving home to cohabitate with strangers, without contact with family and everything else that aids her to feel safe and comfortable.

The Right Place

To relieve this kind of exaggerated (but real to her) anxiety, you will wish to partner with your child to research summer camp options in your community or geographic region. Summer camp also doesn't have to be a place where you stay overnight; it can be a place you visit during the day in order to take advantage of an outdoor activity program. If you present summer camp in an exciting, positive way, your child will be poised to receive the concept with enthusiasm.

Perhaps you went away to summer camp every year yourself. Do you have stories to share about what made it so fun and memorable for you? Did you make long-standing friendships or pen pals as a result of meeting someone special at summer camp?

Know, too, that many communities offer "specialty" summer camp experiences that cater to specific areas of interest (i.e., passions) such as acting and theater, music and musical instruments, gymnastics, soccer, and other athletics to name a few. While most only last several weeks instead of an entire summer, such specialty camps are likely to pique your child's interest, value his passion (and talent!), and offer socialization opportunities with like-minded peers.

Inclusion of children with Asperger's with neurotypical, same-age peers should always be our endeavor. However, in the case of summer camp, you and your child may find relief in an environment in which there are other kids with Asperger's present, and staffed by counselors that are sensitive and respectful of the needs of such kids. This is a personal choice. Finding a camp program near to you that specializes in supporting children with Asperger's may be difficult or even an impossibility. (If you are an impassioned advocate on your child's behalf, you may be the person to collaborate with other parents to officiate the start-up of just such a camp.) Be mindful that it is entirely inappropriate to place your child into an alternate "special-needs" camp because of convenience, staffing ratio, or cost savings. Your child will be miserable in a summer camp for children with mental retardation, for example; and while some camps are strict about entry qualifications, others are not.

DID YOU KNOW?

Your child's success while away at camp—whether it's a day camp or an overnight, away-from-home variety—will likely hinge upon daily structure. Determine in advance the schedule for each day and ensure it is reviewed with your child the night before. Where there are gaps of time, discuss alternatives for your child with him and his counselors.

Choosing a Camp

Aside from the obvious questions about cost and other logistics like administration of medications, water safety, and environmental allergies, you will want to find out the following about any prospective camp to which you are considering sending your child with Asperger's:

- What is the staff to child ratio?
- Do any of the counselors have special education or teaching backgrounds or credits?
- Will your child be assigned to the same counselor(s) for the duration of the summer?
- How often will your child have the opportunity to contact you?
- What is the camp protocol for managing what may be labeled "behaviors" (not just for your kid, but for others that may aggress against your child)?
- What is the camp's policy on bullying?
- Is the camp prepared to accommodate your child's dietary needs?
- What is the structure and routine of a typical day?
- Are children ever left unattended?
- What are the hours during which parents may visit?

You will also wish to meet with the camp director and staff to share information about what works for your child—that is, what makes for a successful day. This can occur without disclosing an Asperger's diagnosis, if you and your child so desire. Also be certain to discuss what's non-negotiable for your child, meaning those adaptations or accommodations he needs to feel safe and comfortable and in control, like knowing the exact time of activities or having his cabin room arranged a certain way. If the non-negotiables become violated, disregarded, or withheld, inform the staff to expect consequences in the form of your child's meltdown or implosion (shutting down), as the case may be.

Preparing for Camp

Obtain a written camp schedule in advance, and give that to your child. Plan to drive with your child to visit the camp in advance of enrollment. Take a camera or camcorder to document the trip. Reviewing the images you've taken of the trip at home will support your child to feel familiar and comfortable with the surroundings. Give him the opportunity to identify what's what to you and others. If siblings, cousins, friends, or others are also going to attend the same camp, find out if they can be paired with your child wherever possible. Arrange for your child to meet the staff and primary counselors, and take their photographs if they'll allow it. Tour the camp-grounds and point out the location of various activity sites. If a living quarters assignment has been made, go there as well and give your child the opportunity to acclimate to it. He will likely be strongly attracted to wooded areas and other local flora and fauna, and this will provide him with an incentive to be there.

An Invaluable Opportunity

Going away to summer camp, either during the day or on a twenty-four-hour-a-day basis, can provide your child with structure during the long hours of summer days. In addition, it may be an opportunity to make social connections with counselors and fellow campers that can be maintained by e-mail or letter writing. Your child may also have the opportunity to learn new skills or demonstrate his own. With careful planning, your child's mind-movie memories of summer camp can be pleasing and every bit as enjoyable as your own.

Chapter 10

Lifelong Lessons

10 Things You Will Learn in this Chapter

- What the single greatest cause of anxiety is in children with Asperger's.

- How making a schedule will help your child (and you) immensely.

- The importance of planning at night.

- How using a "touchstone" of some sort can help soothe your child when he/she is upset.

- To help your child choose the right "touchstone" and teach him/her how to use it.

- Why your child might keep calm and composed all day at school and then have meltdowns at night or on weekends.

- How to empower your child to get out of a situation that he/she is not comfortable in.

- Why acting and music help children flourish.

- How bulleted lists, like cheat sheets, help many kids break complex stories into understandable pieces of information.

- About your child's innate sense of spirituality.

Establishing Schedules

One of the single greatest causes of heightened anxiety in children with Asperger's Syndrome is worries and concerns about the future, that is, not knowing what's coming next. Maintaining control is crucial to kids with Asperger's, and they may become quickly and easily unhinged when routines change without warning or others are privy to information that isn't shared with them or isn't communicated until the last minute. As a result, too many kids with Asperger's are medicated with anxiety-reducing drugs. This is intervention, not prevention; and before such medicine is prescribed, consider implementing any number of the recommendations in this chapter, foremost being the personal schedule.

DID YOU KNOW?

The advantages to supporting your child in initiating a personal schedule are as varied as they are for us all. Our visual daily schedules keep us focused and oriented with respect to time, sequence of events, priorities, and knowledge of what's coming next. Without this structured information we become lost.

None of us is without some sort of long-term time-keeping device, be it a BlackBerry, a calendar (perhaps it's even on your computer desktop), or a hard-copy date book in which you can manually plan for a day, week, or month at a time. Have you ever misplaced your date-keeping device? If so, perhaps you can begin to appreciate the kind of nervous anxiety experienced by those who are at the mercy of others to stay informed of what's upcoming. The longer you go without having your schedule—and knowing you are still responsible for keeping to it—the more upset and distressed you're likely to become. Many people joke that they couldn't function without their schedule and are totally at a loss without it. Why should your child be without a similar way of tracking time and independently assessing impending events and activities? It makes more sense to quell anxiety and foster independent resilience in your child by helping her create a personal schedule.

How to Schedule

Here's how it works: If your child enjoys computers and other electronic equipment, go with him to select an electronic device to suit his needs and interest. If your child handwrites legibly enough for him to read his own writing—and he doesn't mind handwriting— then he may choose to use a hard-copy date book, like a daily, weekly, or monthly planner. In any event, your child should select what appeals to him most, within your budget.

Wherever possible, in partnership with your child, set up the schedule for the next day (at first) the night before. Some parents already spend time tucking their child into bed and, at this time, verbally review the next day; this concept simply builds upon all that good and thoughtful stuff by making it tangible and concrete. Knowing what tomorrow is supposed to "look like" the night before, and having it all recorded so there's no forgetting or mistaking it enables many kids with Asperger's to relax and sleep through the night (when, previously, sleeping well was problematic).

A BETTER PARENTING PRACTICE

If you choose a hard copy book, do not emblazon the outside of it with your child's name and an indication that this is his schedule; that's potentially stigmatizing because it draws unnecessary attention to him.

What to Schedule

The times when the schedule will come in most handy are during those large, unscheduled, unstructured blocks of time like evenings, weekends, holidays, and summer vacation. It will be best to arrange the schedule in a specific sequence if possible. Try setting it up like a "To Do" list that you may use yourself to visually identify what needs to get done and what you've accomplished. Start by scheduling one or two "preferred" activities (these may derive from your child's passions or interests) before scheduling a "nonpreferred" activity, like a household chore or homework. Continue in this sequence—preferred/nonpreferred/preferred—as much as possible. In this way, there is an incentive to use the schedule; there is a sense of accomplishment in visually observing one's achievements; and the schedule isn't perceived as a punitive device used by you to control or manipulate. Fade out your involvement as soon as possible in favor of your child having authority over making the schedule, within parental parameters of course. The schedule may also be used to indicate birthdays, anniversaries, special events, and appointments of all kinds.

Always Go Back to the Schedule

When your child begins to "bug" you with repeated questions, or if she protests or procrastinates about a nonpreferred activity, simply refer back to the schedule—it's all there in black and white. You may suggest, "Well, what does your schedule say is next?" Many such confrontations between parent and child can be nipped in the bud because the child will realize that you can't argue with what's concrete (this doesn't negate occasional parental leniency, as you'd grant any child).

It's probably best not to schedule activities by specific times, unless your child wishes to do so, or you've agreed that Saturday night he can stay up an hour later, for example. Your child may be the type to become exasperated if the schedule isn't maintained to the minute. However, most children with Asperger's find it to be a very useful tool for feeling safe and comfortable and in control of knowing what's coming next.

Using a Touchstone to Soothe

Many people with Asperger's (and autism) soothe themselves by repeatedly manipulating an object such as a straw, a piece of string, or some beads. They find comfort in the sameness of repeating the motion over and over, relishing the calm that the texture of the object in their hand brings. Self-soothing is a strength that should not be misinterpreted or mislabeled. It is used to maintain control, and you'll likely see it intensify when your child is on the verge of losing control, like when she's very happy or excited or angry and upset. It may also kick into high gear if your child is in an environment that is assaulting her senses. You do this too—it just looks a little different, like nervously shaking your leg while seated or persistently chewing on a pen or the inside of your cheek when stressed.

DID YOU KNOW?

The next time you're feeling especially anxious or distressed, try stopping in the moment to assess your outward expression of those feelings. Many people discover themselves unconsciously toying with a ring, a necklace, their hair, or some other device that provides a comforting diversion. This is not unlike the touchstone concept.

Special Touches

Because we are all more alike than different, most of us carry with us a small object that soothes and quells us if we stop to focus on it. Such personal "touchstones" may include a wedding band or favored piece of jewelry, rosary beads or a cross, good luck charms, or photos of loved ones. We carry these objects with us for sentimental reasons or because they hold some significance for us. You may wish to consider offering your child a similar touchstone that will be of lifelong value. The difference here is that of *discretion*, meaning use of the object is secret and private, not public (which may be stigmatizing). The goal here is that the touchstone should remain unseen, such as in a pocket or worn around the neck, under clothing.

Choosing an Object

To begin, ask your child to select a viable touchstone. It will probably be something related to his passion(s), or it might be an object associated with someone with whom he shares a strong, loving bond, such as a grandparent. Advise your child, using words and visuals, that when he is feeling an extreme emotion—but is still in control—he need only touch the object through his clothing, or reach inside a pocket to hold it, and conjure up all that it means to him in the moment. You may use the following story to introduce the concept and modify it to suit your needs:

> People like objects that make them feel comfortable and happy. My (mom/dad/caregiver) uses a _____ in this way. People like to be reminded of other people or things that make them feel happy. Sometimes, I like to think about _____ (the reason for the touchstone). It reminds me of how happy I feel when I _____(engage in the passion).
>
> I can't always _____ (do one's passion), especially when I'm away from home. I can carry _____ (the touchstone) in my pocket to remind me of good times. When I feel anxious or upset, I can touch or hold _____ (the touchstone) to

help me think about _____ (the passion) and
how happy it makes me feel. It's okay to feel anxious
or upset. Everybody feels this way sometimes. By
holding _____ (the touchstone), I may not feel
as anxious or upset.

DOES THIS SOUND LIKE YOUR CHILD?

One young teenager with Asperger's beautifully
demonstrated his understanding that the touchstone is discreet. During a counseling session, he
showed his support team the orange odometer
needle he had selected. But afterward, he privately
approached his counselor to share his other touchstone: a figurine from The Powerpuff Girls cartoon.
He recognized the need to keep the figurine out of
sight and to be selective in showing it to others.

One young man chose to wear a mood ring as his
touchstone. While wearing it was not exactly discreet,
it was still inconspicuous because it was a piece of jewelry typical of other kids his age *and* no one else knew
that he was using it to regulate his own emotions in
the moment, according to the ring's color. It became a
powerful tool for him to maintain control throughout
the day.

The Need to Get Out

Too many children with Asperger's are able to keep com-
posure all day long at school but then come home and
release their pent-up frustration and anxiety in ways that

stun parents and perplex educators who don't notice any difficulties at all during the school day. We all regulate our time by interspersing it with breaks, little rewards and other forms of downtime. These include chatting on the phone, surfing the Internet, using the bathroom, getting a drink or snack, breaking to listen to the radio or watch TV, and other mini-indulgences. Because your child is extremely sensitive, she needs to learn how to pace herself during the day in similar ways in order to avoid becoming so saturated and overwhelmed that she melts down completely upon returning home.

You Can Get Out If You Want

There are very few social situations and environments that you can't extricate yourself from if you so choose. You can even decide to discontinue a dental exam and walk out if you wish. The child with Asperger's Syndrome may not recognize that any other option is available *other than* to remain in the situation—even if it is a situation that is making him feel anxious, upset, and distressed. When it escalates to the point of no return, the child may have a meltdown, shut down, and become unresponsive. Your child *does* have an option to avert public embarrassment and stigmatization through using the "social out."

Empower Your Child

Any of us can go anywhere in the United States and in virtually any situation use the words "Please excuse me," get up, and walk out and have that communication received in a socially acceptable manner. Your child has the right to be empowered with the same under-standing, especially in school where the setting is "gov-erned" by adults adhering to a rigid schedule. Many kids with Asperger's independently figure out how to get their needs met in a similar way; they just do it by going to the water fountain or taking frequent trips to the bathroom. The child who often disappears into the bathroom doesn't have an overactive bladder—he's intelligent enough to have surmised that it's one of the limited opportunities he has to find a relatively calm and quiet place where he can quell anxieties and regroup before going back out into battle.

The Right Words

In collaboration with your child's educational team, teach him to use the words "Please excuse me" or "Excuse me, I need a break." (This will require practice and reminders at first until he gets the hang of it.) It also needs to be understood that his communication will be honored with *immediacy* (this includes you, the par-ent, while in environments outside the home). If your child's communication of the social out is not honored with immediacy but instead with vague statements like, "Hang in there a little bit longer," or "We'll go soon," you've disempowered him and taught him that he really has no control, that, ultimately, adults retain all the control and don't listen.

Using the Social Out

Interpret your child's social out as a strength. What he is really communicating is, "I've held it together for as long as I can, and if we don't get out of here *now*, it's going to get ugly." It is a mark of self-awareness of one's own experience in the moment. It is not about escaping responsibility; don't see it as manipulation.

Once they catch their breath and can process what was happening, most kids will be okay to return to the environment (unless it was overly stimulating). It may *appear* that your child is abusing the social out at first; he's not—your trust is being tested to see if you really will honor it every time. This should fade away as a mutual trust is recognized, but, if not, you might wish to assess your child's environment or the expectations placed upon him in the environment so that adaptations and accommodations may be made.

Expressing Oneself—Acting and Music

Many young people with Asperger's absolutely flourish when given the opportunity to become involved in theater and acting. Many children with Asperger's are naturally brilliant actors and adept mimics, known to entertain others with their dead-on impersonations of TV and cartoon characters. Why not build upon this talent? There is so much to acting that holds special appeal for certain kids:

- You get to become someone other than who you are, which is attractive particularly if you have damaged self-esteem.
- You never say the wrong thing because everything you need to say is already scripted for you.

- If you are challenged in deciphering facial expressions and body language, you get a perfectly acceptable chance to practice understanding such nuances over and over again—it's called rehearsal.
- You are collaborating with others to produce a work of quality.
- There are social connections to be had with others who may be intrigued with or more accepting of others' differences.
- If you're good at what you do, you get positive feedback from your peers or an audience (through applause).

"Movie Talk"

A lot of young people with Asperger's already act every day through using "movie talk." Movie talk (or TV talk) is a skill by which the person has artfully "lifted" lines of dialogue, facial expressions, and even body language from characters in favorite movies, television programs, or cartoon shows and "put it back out" with uncanny accuracy and with all the proper inflections. Many adults with Asperger's have "passed" in life by using movie talk to blend in fairly seamlessly. It is not something to discourage in your child but should be used to facilitate social interactions. The key is not to *become* the fictional character but to assume that character's most socially acceptable traits and make them your own until you feel more comfortable in your own skin. Some folks use movie talk to break the ice in conversation or to initiate an interaction using humor.

▶ A BETTER PARENTING PRACTICE

Do you have a budding actor or actress in your midst? You may notice it early on if you recognize certain movie, cartoon, or TV character dialogue being repeated by your child. Still, one mom needed to counsel her son after he publicly yelled, "Get the hell outta there!" even though its origin was based in movie talk.

It's Her Music

You probably recognized early on in your child's development how listening to her music—favored songs and melodies—was extremely important. (Notice it is *her* music, not the music others choose, which may be violently disconcerting especially if played at uncomfortable decibel levels!) Like acting, all of music is scripted as well. Music therapists know the terms "call" and "response" as they apply to the flow of music. In reading, singing, or playing music, there is a time when one is an active participant in the "conversation." At this time, according to the script, you make your contribution to the song, whether it is through singing or playing an instrument. That's the call. The response comes when, according to the script, you are expected to remain silent and await the reply from one's communication partner(s). Your child may be absolutely passionate about music and performing music. You can use the concept of how music "works" as an analogy for how social conversation is supposed to flow.

Clarity in Writing

The concept of writing stories to aid students to understand social situations and peer conversation was pioneered by a woman named Carol Gray, who is a special education instructor working with kids with different ways of being. She discovered that her students who were especially visual learners had difficulty retaining verbal information and applying it in the context of social settings that would be obvious to most others. For example, one young man didn't understand the concept of raising his hand and waiting to be called upon in class, especially when an instructor stood before the class and asked an open question. The boy didn't realize that the question was not directed to him personally but was being asked of the entire class with the expectation that hands be raised in response. He instead blurted out his responses in ways that were considered socially inept. As you can imagine, this was stigmatizing for him, and his misunderstanding of the situations was interpreted as being deliberately disruptive, which was not the case. Carol Gray resolved this by providing the boy with a brief, bullet-point sequence of sentences that created a story to convey the proper protocol for raising one's hand.

Cheat Sheets

The concept is not unlike the crib notes or "cheat sheets" that many of us have used in school in order to jog our memories in retaining pertinent information. It's the same thing here, and once the boy memorized the story, he was able to automatically remember the proper thing to do and say. Stories such as these are a tangible, concrete way of demystifying the particulars of social situations or environments that may cause apprehension, anxiety, or distress. This strategy has been tremendously successful with children with Asperger's and autism, and you have already seen some similar stories interspersed throughout this book. When you create these stories, it is important to keep in mind the following:

- Keep the stories simple, with a clear beginning and end.
- Follow a clear-cut, logical sequence.
- Try to keep the story to one page in length.
- Don't state anything definitively without allowance for mistakes (we're all human, after all). For example, "I will try to remember to ask to use the CD player." Instead of "I will always remember . . ."
- Allow the story to become your child's personal property to review at her leisure.
- Review it with her regularly outside of the situation that the story was written to explain.
- Fade or discard the story once it's no longer needed.
- The story may be portable but keep it discreetly in a pocket or inside a notebook (or day planner).
- Your child may personalize the story and take a greater interest in "owning" it if she is given the opportunity to illustrate it.

Exploring Spirituality

As a person who may be naturally, inherently gentle and sensitive, your child also may possess an innate sense of spirituality. This doesn't necessarily refer to being religious, but rather spiritual in having a deep appreciation for the beauty in everything and everyone around him. These are the children who are drawn to the tiny details in nature.

DID YOU KNOW?

A 2003 research project conducted by Tanisha Rose, a psychology student at Lincoln University in Philadelphia, examined the stress levels among parents of children with autism. One of Rose's four hypotheses was that as the importance of religion increased, the level of stress experienced by parents would decrease—a factor largely neglected in past stress studies. Rose's study indicated that parents with elevated stress shared a lack of positive religious practices.

Your child's heightened sensitivity may also predispose him to being finely attuned to his environment. He may sense things that others do not—or cannot—readily perceive. If you see this in your child, you've likely seen it from a very early age. Your child may have had powerful dreams, intuitions, or premonitions that proved accurate, or other experiences of a spiritual nature that some would call uncanny coincidences. There are simply some aspects of the human experience that traditional science cannot measure and quantify, like love or faith.

It is important to assume several responsibilities if your child has such heightened sensitivities:

- Accept it as a natural extension of who he is.
- Do not make your child feel in any way unfit or afraid to discuss his sensitivities.
- Do not sensationalize it by exaggerating it, blowing it out of proportion, or openly sharing it with others without your child's knowledge (remember disclosure?).
- Keep it confidential except to reveal information to those who can be trusted to understand unconditionally.
- Remember that intermittent experiences do not a mental illness make. Review the mental health chapter again if you have concerns; common mental health diagnoses are determined by groupings of symptoms, not by sporadic, unexplainable instances.
- Accept what your child tells you to be the truth as he knows it.

As your child enters adolescence and adulthood, his sense of spirituality and commitment of faith to a higher authority may be the very thing that pulls him through rough times. Having these values instilled in him early on in life could prove to be his single most important resource.

Chapter 11

You: An Asperger's Parent

10 Things You Will Learn in this Chapter

- What are typical parental reactions and what are not.

- How questions like "why me" are normal but unhelpful.

- About different ways of looking at a diagnosis—
  were you meant to be the parent of a child with
  Asperger's?

- How to spot little messages of love that your child
  is trying to send you.

- How making a list of things you've learned about
  Asperger's is a powerful tool.

- How to do more in your community if you want.

- About parameters of the current federal, state,
  and local service systems available to children with
  differences.

- How your child's reality will change as he/she
  grows into adulthood.

- Why you should stop using the term politically correct and think in terms of personal respect instead.

- How your child can teach you to be a better
  person.

What Have You Learned?

Think back to the moment you first received your child's
diagnosis of Asperger's Syndrome. What were you feeling in that moment? Confusion? Upset? Despair?
Hopelessness? Next, think about how you're feeling
now, today, especially after having read this book. How
much differently do you feel now compared to then?

You and your child have been on quite a journey
together. He or she has worked to adapt to people,
places, and things that are often very difficult to discern
without your gentle support and guidance. Your child
has come a long way toward becoming more self-suffi-
cient and independent. But what about you? What have
you learned as an Asperger's parent? One mom, Gina,
eloquently summarizes her thoughts and feelings in a
way that many parents will relate to best.

I've always thought of having a child with Asperger's
Syndrome as a journey. It begins with the never-to-
be-forgotten moment the words tumble out of a
physician's mouth. Little do any of us realize it at
the time, but the whole world is about to change
forever. Sometimes there is grief, sometimes despair.
Yet there are also times of such profound revelation,
such profound love, that you find yourself thank-
ing God that He gave you this incredible being who
inevitably expanded you and taught you so much.

In the early days, I remember thinking, "Why
me? Why Jon?" One day the answer came to me.
"Why *not* me? Why not my son?" If there was to be a
child with Asperger's, perhaps I was the perfect per-

son to be that child's parent. And perhaps I needed that child just as much as he needed me. I am forever changed because of it. And I cannot imagine being anyone but the person I am today. If Jon is a special-needs kid, then maybe *I'm* a special-needs parent.

A BETTER PARENTING PRACTICE

Are you someone who believes that everything happens for a reason, or that our destinies are predetermined? If so, the quote from Gina about her son should have special resonance. Has your role as a parent been reversed, and were you the person with the special need prior to your child being in your life? Food for thought.

Another equally wise mother shared her observations as well:

Your job, like Edison's mother, is to develop the child's potential, which may be greater (or not) than your own. You are helping him to unlock his world. You deepen your relationship with the child. He may share some insights only with you, about himself or about what he is learning or creating. What a privilege!

Bonnie believes in using her son Noel's passions in order to gain access to his way of thinking. Not only has this made the teaching and learning process easier and more effective, she has had the pleasure of seeing her son learn and achieve. In so doing, Bonnie has found that she's learned a lot about herself, and calls the special bond with Noel "an amazing experience."

Without your child in your life, you would be a different person, wouldn't you? As the parent of a child with Asperger's Syndrome, how has your life been "forever changed"? Perhaps you have become stronger, more vocal, or more defensive in protection of your child and her rights. (By extension, are you more tolerant and compassionate of differences in people of all kinds?) Perhaps your example of total, loving acceptance has been the model others follow, including your other children. Remember that your child will reflect back to you what you project upon her. Armed with your loving support, your trust and your confidence, your child will be poised for great things. And you have every reason to expect them.

Share Your Knowledge

Like all human beings, you have likely done or said hurtful things to your child out of frustration or exasperation. This is typical of any parent, not just the parent of a child with Asperger's. But have you found yourself in a rut? Do you still see the glass as half empty? You may find yourself asking, "Why me?" Your frustration may stem from your child's limitations or your own challenge to cope day to day. You may wish your child would "snap out of it" and get with the "program." Shouldn't your child figure out how to fit in and make a go of it, just like anyone else who's ever had any kind of challenge in life? This question may be answered with another question that will prompt some self-reflection: What do you think your child has been doing all this time?

Little Messages of Love

Your child has a great desire to give back to you and others. If you are a parent who has been blocked by myths and stereotypes, you may well have missed the times your child has reached out to you. It can be very subtle and may come when you least expect it, like the child who made his dad a leading character in his hand-drawn comic strips.

A BETTER PARENTING PRACTICE

As a simple exercise, develop a written list of all the things you've learned from your child with Asperger's Syndrome. The list may include items that are academic in nature, inspired by her most passionate of interests, or lessons about sensitivity toward others, or patience. It may be a powerful thing to lovingly share your list with your child, perhaps at a special event like a sixteenth or twenty-first birthday or a graduation.

Most parents simply want their child to be happy. Your child has a lot to offer you as well as the rest of the world; and he has every reason to assume his rightful place in the world and be recognized for his contributions. The two most important things you can do for your child with Asperger's are to value, encourage, and indulge his most passionate interests (with an eye toward a future vocation), and foster the development of a relationship with at least one ally. In so doing, your child will be better poised to prosper in life.

Asperger's in the World Today

As we learn more about autism and Asperger's Syndrome, a burgeoning community of support has developed. Parents are no longer content to accept the oftentimes very limiting parameters of the current federal, state, and local service systems available to children with differences. Instead they are becoming impassioned advocates, creating in-roads, shaping laws, and dictating what is and what is not acceptable for their children. As you've learned, parents have long established formal and informal local networks, accessible through state and county social service systems. A resource list, included at the back of this book, highlights some of the many online Asperger's Syndrome groups organized to educate, enlighten, and entertain individuals, families, friends, and the community.

Adapting as an Adult

Your child, teenager, or young adult with Asperger's may feel isolated and estranged from others who share his similarities. Forging friendships with like others is a personal choice that may be of little to no consequence to your child, especially if he is comfortable with the number of healthy relationships in his life. Still others seek a kinship that may not be readily found in one's hometown. Computer technology and the Internet has revolutionized our world, and, in particular, has been a blessing for the person with Asperger's Syndrome for reasons previously outlined. It is entirely possible for your child to communicate with others around the world that are also seeking a connectedness in learning about Asperger's Syndrome and themselves.

DID YOU KNOW?

We are still a long way from achieving a perfect system for individuals with mental retardation, autism, and other ways of being. In seeking formal and informal supports for your child, don't be surprised if you are both a recipient of service and an educator to others. Many traditional services are based on a medical or mental retardation model, and not an autism or Asperger's service delivery model. As always, encourage your child to be his own best advocate.

From the comfort of one's home, your child can converse with others; understand more about herself; feel joy and relief in comparing daily challenges others face; and vent about the general intolerance of the "big world." Through these relationships, your child may develop an enhanced confidence and comfort level about Asperger's—it's really *not* so different after all. Opportunities to meet in person, to make formal presentations, or to contribute to various online and hard-copy publications may be available. It is a rare individual with Asperger's who does not desire to educate others.

What the Future Holds

Ultimately, we are all temporary in the lives of the people that we know and love. After you have passed on, your wish for your child may include that she be surrounded with a circle of loved ones and friends, to be successfully employed, and to be well accepted—if not revered—in her chosen community. Hopefully, this introduction to Asperger's Syndrome has provided you with philosophies and strategies that match well with your role as a parent. Use what makes sense and leave behind what does not. You may wish to use this book as a springboard to others that are more specific and technical, or you may wish to read about those who have encountered, lived with, or loved someone with Asperger's Syndrome.

▶ DID YOU KNOW?

If you've enjoyed (and could relate to) the personal stories and anecdotes sprinkled throughout this book, you are certain to relish the unique and innovative perspectives of those who have so eloquently made written record of their experiences. Some such biographies are listed in Appendix A.

As we look to the future, we are seeing a growing acceptance in our culture of *all* people with different ways of being. Our language used to describe people's differences is no longer a matter of "political correctness," it is a show of renewed respect. In this day and age, no one can justly define "normal" or "typical." Not one of us can say we don't know someone with a difference or disability. This may include the woman who's had a mastectomy, the man who developed Parkinson's disease, the teenager with an eating disorder, or the child with Down Syndrome. At some point in time, we will collectively recognize that *all* ways of being, including Asperger's Syndrome, are simply a normal part of being human. After all, we're all more alike than different.

Appendix A

Further Reading

Aston, Maxine. *Asperger's in Love: Couple Relationships and Family Affairs* (London: Jessica Kingsley Publishers, Ltd., 2003).

Attwood, Tony. *Asperger's Syndrome: A Guide For Parents and Professionals* (London: Jessica Kingsley Publishers, Ltd., 1998).

Birch, Jen. *Congratulations! It's Asperger Syndrome* (London: Jessica Kingsley Publishers, Ltd., 2003).

Boyd, Brenda. *Parenting a child with Asperger syndrome: 200 Tips and Strategies* (London: Jessica Kingsley Publishers, Ltd., 2003).

Cohen, Shirley. *Targeting Autism* (Berkeley: University of California Press, 1998).

Faherty, Catherine. *Asperger's: What Does It Mean to Me? Structured Teaching Ideas for Home and School* (Arlington, TX: Future Horizons Inc., 2000).

Grandin, Temple. *Thinking in Pictures and Other Reports from My Life with Autism* (New York: Doubleday, 1995).

Gray, Carol. *The Original Social Story Book* (Arlington, TX: Future Horizons, Inc., 1994).

_____. *The New Social Story Book: Illustrated Edition* (Arlington, TX: Future Horizons, Inc., 2000).

Holliday Willey, Liane. *Pretending to be Normal: Living with Asperger's Syndrome* (London: Jessica Kingsley Publishers, Ltd., 1999).

_____. *Asperger Syndrome in the Family* (London: Jessica Kingsley Publishers, Ltd., 2001).

Jackson, Luke. *Freaks, Geeks and Asperger's Syndrome: A User's Guide to Adolescence* (London: Jessica Kingsley Publishers, Ltd., 2002).

Kephart, Beth. *A Slant of Sun: One Child's Courage* (New York: W.W. Norton & Company, Inc., 1998).

Lawson, Wendy. *Build Your Own Life: A Self-Help Guide for Individuals with Asperger's Syndrome* (London: Jessica Kingsley Publishers. Ltd., 2003).

Meyer, Roger. *Asperger Syndrome Employment Workbook: An Employment Workbook for Adults with Asperger Syndrome* (London: Jessica Kingsley Publishers. Ltd., 2000).

Moyes, Rebecca A. *Incorporating Social Skills in the Classroom: A Guide for Teachers and Parents of Children with High-Functioning Autism and Asperger Syndrome* (London: Jessica Kingsley Publishers. Ltd., 2001).

_____. *Addressing the Challenging Behavior of Children with High-Functioning Autism/Asperger Syndrome in the Classroom: A Guide for Teachers and Parents* (London: Jessica Kingsley Publishers. Ltd., 2002).

Nash, J. Madelene, "The Secrets of Autism," *Time*, 6 May 2002.

O'Neill, Jasmine Lee. *Through the Eyes of Aliens: A Book About Autistic People* (London: Jessica Kingsley Publishers, Ltd., 1999).

Papolos, Demitri F., and Janice Papolos. *The Bipolar Child: The Definitive and Reassuring Guide to Childhood's Most Misunderstood Disorder* (New York: Broadway Books, 1999).

Pary, Robert J., MD, Andrew S. Levitas, MD, and Anne DesNoyers Hurley, PhD. "Diagnosis of Bipolar Disorder in Persons with Developmental Disabilities," *Mental Health Aspects of Developmental Disabilities*, vol. 2, no. 2, April/May/June 1999.

Pyles, Lise. *Hitchhiking through Asperger Syndrome: How to Help Your Child When No One Else Will* (London: Jessica Kingsley Publishers, Ltd., 2001).

Ryan, Ruth, MD. *Handbook of Mental Health Care for Persons with Developmental Disabilities* (Denver, CO: Omnipress, 1999).

Stanford, Ashley. *Asperger Syndrome and Long-Term Relationships* (London: Jessica Kingsley Publishers, Ltd., 2002).

Stillman, William. *Demystifying the Autistic Experience: A Humanistic Introduction for Parents, Caregivers and Educators* (London: Jessica Kingsley Publishers, Ltd., 2002).

Unok-Marks, Susan, Carl Schrader, Mark Levine, Chris Hagie, Trish Longaker, Maggie Morales, and Iris Peters. "Social Skills for Social Ills: Supporting the Social Skills Development of Adolescents with Asperger's Syndrome," *Teaching Exceptional Children*, November/December 1999.

Winter, Matt. *Asperger's Syndrome: What Teachers Need to Know* (London: Jessica Kingsley Publishers, Ltd., 2003).

Resources

www.aane.org
Asperger's Association of New England that fosters awareness, respect, acceptance, and support for people with Asperger's and their families.

www.aspennj.org
Asperger Syndrome Education Network, Inc., headquartered in New Jersey.

www.aspergersyndrome.org
Online Asperger's Syndrome Information and Support (OASIS), site created by parents.

www.autismservicescenter.org
The Autism Service Center, a national autism hotline and Web site.

www.autism-society.org
Autism Society of America.

www.ed.gov
United States Department of Education Web site.

www.feat.org
Families for Early Autism Treatment.

www.maapservices.org
Covers autism, Asperger's Syndrome, and pervasive developmental disorder.

www.nacdd.org
National Association of Councils on Developmental Disabilities.

www.ninds.nih.gov/disorders/autism/autism.htm
National Institutes of Health autism site.

www.P2PUSA.org
National Parent to Parent Network Web site.

www.transitionmap.org
A Web site by Pennsylvania professionals for educators supporting high school students with differences who are transitioning to adult life.

www.unlockingautism.org
The Unlocking Autism Web site with a listserv to connect parents, teens, and adults with autism and Asperger's.

www.wrightslaw.org
The Web site of Peter Wright, Esquire, an expert on special education.

http://policeandautism.cjb.net/avoiding.html
A Web page about autism and law enforcement.

Index